HEAL THE HURT

DR ANN MACASKILL MA, AFBPS, C.PSYCHOL is a reader in psychology and Director of the Centre for Research on Human Behaviour at Sheffield Hallam University as well as being a Chartered Health Psychologist. She has been trained in counselling and cognitive behaviour therapy. She carries out research in the area of forgiveness and has published extensively in psychology journals and books on psychotherapy, treatment for depression, stress, health and forgiveness. She has appeared on television and made many radio broadcasts.

NETWORK for CHANGE LTD.
150-152 LONDON ROAD
LEICESTER LE2 1ND
Tel: 0116 2470335
Fax: 0116 2470766
email: info@networkforchange.org.uk

Overcoming Common Problems Series

For a full list of titles please contact
Sheldon Press, 1 Marylebone Road, London NW1 4DU

Overcoming Common Problems Series

Overcoming Common Problems Series

Overcoming Common Problems

Heal the Hurt

How to Forgive and Move on

Dr Ann Macaskill

First published in Great Britain in 2002 by
Sheldon Press
1 Marylebone Road
London NW1 4DU

British Library Cataloguing-in-Publication Data

A catalogue record for this book is available from the British Library

ISBN 0–85969–882–3

Typeset by Deltatype Limited, Birkenhead, Merseyside
Printed in Great Britain by
Biddles Ltd, *www.biddles.co.uk*

Contents

PART ONE:
UNDERSTANDING FORGIVENESS

1

Introduction

Human beings appear to have an infinite capacity to hurt one another. Sometimes the hurt is intentional; at other times it is caused by circumstances or misunderstandings. Whatever the cause, forgiveness of the hurt caused is not something that comes easily to most people and we can carry grudges and hurts for many years. In the course of my professional life I have seen many people who are harbouring hurts that they have carried for years. It can be very difficult to forgive, but we frequently underestimate the pain and stress caused to ourselves, and those around us, by failing to forgive and holding grudges. How often in conversation do we hear, 'I'll never forgive him/her for that. As long as I live, I shall never forgive or forget what they have done to me.' Frequently rifts occur and people end up never talking to one another again.

As a psychologist I find myself asking about the costs in terms of personal grief, ill-health and loneliness of non-forgiveness. Is holding a grudge, nursing a hurt, really worth the associated pain, the feeling of being stuck in the past, unable to move on? Does it really have any effect on the person or persons who committed the perceived wrong, or is the pain one-sided? Is it simply the victim that continues to hurt? If this is the case, and I suggest that it is in most instances, surely it is better to try to work towards some resolution of the grief, hurt and/or anger, even if total forgiveness is not possible or even desirable? It may be that some things are impossible to forgive, but continuing to suffer deeply from the wrong done to one means that in a sense the wrongdoer is still 'winning', in that they continue to affect the victim's life, day in and day out.

This book aims to explore some of the factors that influence how we feel when we have been wronged in some way. It examines the position we find ourselves in with regard to the person who has committed the wrongdoing. This allows us to reflect on our feelings about the situation and to consider over time other aspects of this situation and to decide what is really best for us, our long-term health and our future. We explore some of the stages of this process of forgiveness, identifying the work that has to be done and suggesting ways of tackling this, using case study examples to illustrate when appropriate. Where forgiveness is not considered an achievable state, we look at how this can best be handled psychologically to try to minimize the negative impact on future functioning and well-being.

At each step in the process there are exercises to help isolate our concerns, identify our feelings and explore whether forgiveness may be a possibility, something that with help we can work towards. You may find some of these exercises difficult or painful to complete, but if you stick with it you will come to better understand your own situation and arrive at a position where it will be possible to work towards forgiveness. It is not intended that this is a quick fix. You may have spent a long time harbouring feelings of hurt and resentment and you have to be prepared to work hard to change these feelings. You need to keep telling yourself that by continuing to hold on to your hurts and grudges you are undoubtedly damaging yourself. It is quite likely that you are the person who is hurting most! The person who you feel wronged you is in all probability getting on with their life, seldom if ever giving you a second thought. You owe it to yourself to try for some resolution of your feelings so that you can begin to lead a happier and more fulfilling life.

It is difficult to know exactly how to talk about individuals who have been hurt and the people who have done the hurting. For simplicity, and to aid discussion, I use the words *victim* and *perpetrator* when discussing forgiveness. These are frequently seen as emotionally-laden, blaming terms, but this is certainly not intended here. Indeed, there may be many instances where it is extremely difficult to apportion blame or guilt, even if it were helpful to do so. Nevertheless individuals are likely to have identified themselves as either the victim or the perpetrator, and so these are the terms I use. Pragmatically it does not matter if both parties see themselves as victims in the early stages of the process, as long as there is a wish to proceed towards forgiveness. Also in the course of the text I address issues relevant to both the victim and the perpetrator. Again for simplicity, I write as if there were only two individuals in the process. In reality there may of course be more than one person involved, either as the perpetrator or the victim, or indeed it may be racial or religious groups or institutions on a large scale that have left us feeling hurt or angry at the way we have been treated.

Within a religious context and in the Christian tradition particularly, great emphasis is placed on divine forgiveness. This is sought through a process of confession, repentance, praying for forgiveness and atoning for the sins committed. The emphasis here is on the wrongdoer and their relationship with God. Some individuals may feel that divine forgiveness is all that is important for their long-term happiness and well-being. I would argue, however, that in the interests of human happiness we need to focus some of our energies on fostering interpersonal and intergroup forgiveness. Throughout human history we can see the devastating effects of human non-forgiveness, grudge-holding and attempts at retribution in terms of wars, strife and inter-racial conflict. Therefore while accepting that divine forgiveness is extremely important and helpful for some individuals, here I focus on human interpersonal forgiveness and forgiveness of self. We identify the steps individuals can take to become more forgiving people. The emphasis is mainly on the victim, although later in the book issues around the perpetrator emerge.

2

The nature of forgiveness: understanding the process

What is meant by forgiveness?

Forgiveness is not easy to define. There are degrees of forgiveness; as an initial working definition I suggest that achieving a state of forgiving involves giving up feelings of hurt and ill-will towards the perpetrator, and no longer being preoccupied with the hurtful event, spending significant amounts of time thinking about it. Forgiveness can be said to have truly occurred when the individual begins to pick up the threads of their life and starts moving forwards in a healthy, constructive way. The victim no longer spends large chunks of time dwelling on the wrongdoing, constantly bringing it to mind in situations which bear similarities to the one in which it originally occurred. Forgiveness in most instances involves forgoing vengeful behaviour. This may be achieved by truly forgiving, or by coming to feel that the perpetrator will 'get their just deserts' at some time in the future.

This is a somewhat oversimplified summary of the psychological processes involved, but it allows us to appreciate the complexity of the whole process. It is due to this complexity that forgiveness seldom occurs quickly; most people have to work hard at achieving it. Many of the people I talk to initially believe that having said to the perpetrator, 'I forgive you,' they have truly forgiven them. However, as this example shows, a public statement of forgiveness is often just the first step in the process. Indeed frequently it has little to do with real forgiveness; rather, what the individual is doing is making a commitment to try to work towards forgiveness.

Sue's partner of ten years, John, had been unfaithful to her with a friend of hers. The illicit relationship had initially begun at a party. Sue had felt unwell and left the party early, but she had insisted that John stay, as he was having a good time. He got on very well with Petra, they shared a taxi home and he went in for coffee. The next day she rang him at work, they arranged to meet and an affair began. The relationship continued for several weeks, until John ended it, realizing that he loved Sue and did not want to jeopardize their future together. Petra was very unhappy at the ending of the affair and told Sue all about it. She blamed the end of the relationship on Sue's dependency on John – she said John wanted to leave Sue but was afraid of what Sue would do if he did. Sue confronted John and asked him to leave, which he did, returning to live at his parents' house.

Sue then discovered she was pregnant. She informed John, and they started to see each other again. After several weeks of discussion, John moved back in and they appeared to have resolved their problems. Sue emphatically stated that she had forgiven John – they were looking forward to the baby and getting on with their lives. However, difficulties remained which were exacerbated by the birth of the baby. One year later they found their way into counselling. To summarize what was discussed, John stated that Sue, while claiming to have forgiven him for his infidelity, kept bringing it up every time they had even a minor disagreement. If he was just a few minutes late home, or if he wanted to go to the pub with his mates, she would make comments about his past relationship, and he always had to specify precisely when he would be back.

Sue agreed that she felt she could not trust him. He seemed to expect everything to be the same between them as it had been previously, but that was asking too much of her. She felt that it was easy for him. While agreeing that he was good with the baby, and that many things had improved, she came to realize that she had not really forgiven John for the hurt he had caused her. She thought he had 'got off lightly', and it did appear from some of her behaviour that she was still intent on punishing him. There was a feeling that he had not been remorseful enough and needed to be made to suffer. John had gone along with this at first, because he felt guilty, but he felt that, two years on, the incident should be allowed to die.

With help, Sue and John came to see that they still had a lot of work to do before Sue could really say that she had forgiven him. Her initial statement of forgiveness had merely been the first stage in the process. She had made a commitment to work towards trying to forgive him but was unaware she had some way to go to achieve this. However, John had taken her at her word, and truly believed himself to be forgiven – hence his outrage two years later when his infidelity was still a constant topic in their interactions.

We will discuss later in the book ways that such difficulties can be overcome, but the point of this example is to emphasize the difficulty of attaining true forgiveness. For most people, to say that they have forgiven the perpetrator is not sufficient. The verbal expression of forgiveness is normally just the first step in the process. It is a commitment to forgive, where most people are really saying, 'I would like to be able to forgive you, and I will try.' A lot of other things, including the passage of time, may have to occur before true forgiveness is achieved. Difficulties occur when the true complexity of the forgiveness process is not acknowledged or understood, on either side, as in the case of Sue and John.

It may be useful for our understanding of the processes involved to distinguish forgiveness from other related behaviours, to ensure that we are working with a joint understanding of what is involved in forgiveness.

Pardoning is generally a legal term, implying that technically forgiveness has occurred, but it has little to do with interpersonal forgiveness. People can receive official pardons but may not be able to forgive themselves for something they have done.

Condoning is another term sometimes confused with forgiveness. When some wrongdoing is condoned, this can imply that the perpetrator was in some way justified in committing the offence. We sometimes become aware of people condoning when they say things like, 'I know what he did was wrong but there has been a bad history between them. He has not always been the guilty party, and you can only be expected to take so much.'

Excusing is similar to condoning. We accept that the person had a good reason for behaving as they did. Legally there have been instances of this: women who after suffering years of abuse from their partner have suddenly fought back. In at least one incident the abusing male has been fatally wounded. The history of abuse is perceived as a mitigating circumstance and the woman inflicting the fatal wound may be treated less harshly. There is an element of excusing the crime because of the earlier prolonged provocation. Again, this is not forgiveness, but the psychological processes involved can be quite similar to, and even an integral part of, the forgiveness process. Evidence shows, however, that even when wrongdoing has been condoned or pardoned, issues of forgiveness may still remain.

People often ask whether reconciliation with the wrongdoer is necessary for forgiveness to have been truly achieved. This is patently not the case. You can come to forgive someone you are no longer in

8

contact with, either through choice or because of geographical distance. Indeed, you may even come to forgive someone who is dead. This may be a very worthwhile undertaking.

Amanda had been severely abused by a close male relative during her childhood. This relative, an uncle, was long deceased, but his influence lived on in the way Amanda lived her life. She was in her late twenties, an extremely unhappy young woman who was unable to commit to any long-term relationship with a male. She could not trust men, seeing in every man she met the potential for the abusing relationship she had experienced with her uncle to develop. Yet she desperately longed for a close loving relationship. Only by laying the ghost of her dead uncle and coming to understand why he acted as he did, could she finally begin to give up the past hurts and move on. At the end of a long struggle she came to see the futility of holding on to her anger and resentment and was able to get on with her life. It is debatable whether complete forgiveness is ever possible under such circumstances, but certainly Amanda developed a different interpretation of her past experience, and while she couldn't excuse her uncle's behaviour she began to see where it had come from in his past. She changed from hating him to pitying him, from seeing him as a bully, who always got what he wanted in life, to a psychologically flawed person who ultimately had a very unhappy life. By letting go of the anger and ceasing to focus on the past, she was able, with help, to move on to a more positive future and eventually stop seeing the potential for every man she met to become her bullying uncle.

Why is forgiveness so complex and difficult?

As we are beginning to see, forgiveness is a complex process, the endpoint of a developmental sequence of behaviours beginning with the original wrong. It is something that normally takes time to achieve. We have to be willing to work at it. By exploring the process we can begin to understand why this is the case.

The original wrongdoing generates a whole gamut of emotions. There is the initial state of *shock* that the wrongdoing has happened. This is generally accompanied by feelings of *disbelief*, a sense of unreality. The victim feels that there must have been some mistake –

this cannot possibly be happening to them, they will wake up and realize it is a dream, and so on. There will be accompanying feelings of *hurt* and *anger*. How dare the perpetrator treat them in this way, they have done nothing to deserve this. Underlying this anger and hurt there is frequently an element of *fear*. This is not always immediately apparent or acknowledged but nevertheless it plays an important part in determining our responses when we have been hurt in this way. We need to explore where some of this fear originates.

As human beings, we are social animals. We need other people. Interacting with others gives us pleasure and we develop all sorts of interdependencies with them. We feel good when other people are nice to us. In psychological terms this is conceptualized as human beings having high needs for positive regard from others. However, this need for positive regard from other people has a downside. It makes us vulnerable, as it gives other people power over us. Think how much easier it is to accept praise rather than criticism. How often do we end up doing something that we may not really want to do, just so that others will continue to think well of us and will not criticize us? We do not want to be thought difficult or unhelpful. This need for positive regard frequently exerts a powerful influence on our actions; it stops us doing things we may want to do for fear of its withdrawal. It also means that we assume others will operate using the same rules as we do, so we are surprised when people behave badly towards us. We do not expect betrayals and wrongdoing from those we habitually interact with.

All relationships involve a significant element of trust. When we meet someone new we tend to take them at face value and reserve judgement until we know more about them. Once we know someone, we usually function with them on the basis that we expect the best from them. If we are fair to others we expect them to reciprocate. Wrongdoing violates this basic trust. It can profoundly disturb our faith in other human beings and make us less trusting in our dealings with others. Feeling that one has been betrayed or treated unjustly by a perpetrator brings home to us how in all our interactions we give other people power over us – the power to hurt us and treat us unjustly, be it anything from relatively harmless gossip to more extreme cases of serious abuse of some kind.

This results in our experiencing fear. What has happened to us once may happen again. We want to protect ourselves, and this need for protection may result in us becoming reluctant to interact with others, maybe even avoiding any close relationships. However, for most of us social isolation is unsatisfying and likely to be in any case unattainable. We live and work surrounded by people, and for our own psychological well-being we need to be able to relate appropriately to others. This means that we need to be able to trust. When we are betrayed or treated badly, this basic trust in others that we all have is violated. This violation of trust is one of the fundamental barriers to forgiveness. An example will make this clearer.

Stuart met Dianne at a ballroom dancing club. Stuart had been happily married for 20 years but his wife had died the previous year. He was just beginning to come to terms with his grief, pick up the pieces and create a new social life for himself, hence the ballroom dancing class. Dianne was a few years younger than him, an attractive divorcee who had moved into the area fairly recently. The relationship flourished, and they went on an expensive holiday together, paid for by Stuart. Shortly after the holiday, Dianne said that there was some problem with the lease of her flat and she would have to find somewhere else to live. Stuart suggested she move in with him in the short term. They could then make decisions about the future once they saw how they got along living together. They had known each other for five months at this point.

Then Stuart had to go away on business for three weeks and he left Dianne to take care of his home during this time. He arranged for her to have access to his finances while he was away so that she could deal with any bills. On returning home, imagine his consternation to find no Dianne, and his house cleared of anything of value, including his dead wife's jewellery. His bank account had been emptied. There was no letter of explanation, she had simply disappeared. The police were notified and it transpired that the woman he had known as Dianne was a fraudster with a previous history. She worked with a male accomplice and befriended vulnerable men, recently widowed or divorced, who were all fairly wealthy. Having worked her way into their affections she disappeared when a suitable opportunity arose with as many of their valuables as she could easily remove. Stuart felt utterly betrayed. He had trusted this woman, believing he had a good honest relationship with her, and it was all lies! As well as the hurt and anger, his fundamental confidence in his own ability to judge people was shattered. The question he kept asking was, 'How do I ever trust a woman again?'

While this is a particularly dramatic example of betrayal of trust, it does make us recognize the important part that trust plays in our interactions with others. Every time we meet someone new we take him or her on trust. Every time someone we know tells us something we trust it to be true. Every encounter in our lives is based on an implicit assumption that people are as they seem, they are not intending to deceive us and they can be trusted, to some extent at least. When this trust is betrayed it is as if the rug has been pulled out from under us. We can lose confidence in our own judgement and become crippled in social situations or restrict our lives to the known and familiar. Enormous hurt, and also anger, generally accompanies this betrayal. Some people focus on their anger and may try to deny that the hurt exists. Generally, though, it is hurt that fuels their anger.

To help us better comprehend the importance of trust it is worth spending a little time looking at its origins in our development. The consensus in psychological literature is that one of the mains tasks, if not the main task, of early childhood is to develop this basic trust in other human beings that allows us to interact successfully with other people. The way that this occurs is relatively straightforward. The young infant is totally dependent on the adults in its world to provide for its needs. When the baby is hungry she cries and one of her carers picks her up and she is fed. Similarly if the baby has a wet nappy, an adult changes her and makes her comfortable. If the baby is afraid and cries, again she is picked up and comforted. In this way babies quickly learn that the adults in their environment can be relied on to meet their needs, comfort them when they are afraid, feed them when they are hungry, take away discomfort and generally be there when they want them. If our needs are met in this way we learn to trust other people as they make our world a relatively safe, predictable place that meets our needs. Problems only arise when the infant is surviving in an unpredictable world, where their needs are not reliably met. This is the experience of the child who is abused. Adults may ignore them when they are hungry, upset or in discomfort. Worse still, adults may be the source of pain and discomfort for the abused child. Adults in these circumstances do not behave in predictable ways and the child in this instance learns to mistrust others and learns that the world is a very unpredictable and frequently hostile place.

Most of us, however, are fortunate enough when we are growing up to have our needs met by our carers and we develop this basic trust in other people that allows us to go out into the world, meet new people, make friends and have lasting relationships. We frequently operate, albeit unconsciously, according to the maxim, 'Do unto others as you would wish them to do unto you.' We do not go through life lying to others, betraying them and generally treating them badly, so we do not expect others to do this to us. We operate on the basis of trust in our interactions with others. Hence our distress when we feel that this trust has been abused in some way. In these circumstances forgiveness is not usually the first response that most of us have, as the case studies illustrate. We are shocked, hurt, angry, afraid; a whole range of emotions is experienced, causing us high levels of distress.

We need to explore this process further to understand what we might go through when we feel we have been wronged. When it actually happens to us we are generally too distressed to be able to analyse and recognize accurately the psychological processes we are experiencing. We examine here what actually occurs in some detail.

Making judgements about the severity of wrongdoing

When wrongdoing occurs, the victim comes to some conclusion about the severity of what has happened. We tend to do this very automatically and so are not conscious of the processes involved. There are various factors that may influence our judgement, depending to some extent on the situation we find ourselves in, but it is certain that a judgement is made about the degree of wrong carried out by the perpetrator. Here, as elsewhere, individual personality characteristics play a part in determining the nature of the decision-making process. A relaxed individual is likely to be less offended by the same incident than is someone who is very concerned with observing social proprieties.

Victims consider many factors and make decisions about them before coming to a judgement about the perceived severity of wrongdoing against them. I have used the phrase 'perceived severity' advisedly, as it is important to stress at the outset that all these judgements are relative and it is very helpful to keep focusing on that. Frequently victims become even more hurt and enraged when others in their lives do not share their exact interpretations of the wrongdoing. It is important to accept that each of us sees the world from our own perspective, and this will be heavily influenced by our personality, past experience, needs and present emotional state, among other things.

Confronted by a novel situation when we have to decide how to react, we are likely to make a tentative judgement and then check it out with our friends. For example, imagine you are invited to attend a garden party to meet the Queen. You take advice on a suitable dress code and probably discuss your choice with friends. (This situation possibly applies more to women than men.) The difficulty involved in dealing with the novelty of the situation is acknowledged by your women friends with such comments as, 'It's easier for men. They just wear a suit.' Our tentative decisions are then sounded out with family and friends. We are looking to obtain confirmation that our initial judgement was correct. If that is not the case, we may add a hat or alter the outfit in some other way until a consensus is reached that we are properly dressed for the occasion. This process then gives us the confidence that we are behaving appropriately. In this instance, we started with our perception of an appropriate dress code, checked our perception against significant others in our lives and then came to a final conclusion.

A similar process occurs when we are making judgements about perceived wrongdoing. We will now unpick this process and explore its constituent parts.

The following list describes the main factors that victims consider and make decisions about when coming to a judgement about the perceived severity of wrongdoing against them.

- *The degree of the perceived wrong.* On a scale from massive to trivial, where is this offence?
- *The amount of distress engendered by the wrongdoing.* On a scale from major to minor, what is the emotional impact of the transgression?
- *The perceived intentionality of the transgression.* It may be perceived to be accidental, in which case it is judged less severely, with less direct blame on the perpetrator. It could be the result of negligence and here there is likely to be some more direct blaming of the perpetrator – they should have been more careful. If it is judged to be intentional, then it will be rated as severe.
- *An assessment of the quantity of wrongdoing.* Consideration is given to the way the perpetator has behaved towards the victim and others in the past. If this appears to be an isolated incident it is likely to be viewed less severely than if it is part of a frequently observed pattern of behaviour on the perpetrator's part. Historical factors may be

particularly salient when considering perceived wrongdoing that has an inter-group aspect to it.

- *The nature of the previous relationship between the victim and the perpetrator.* The relevant features are likely to be the closeness of the relationship and its length.
- *Any mitigating circumstances that may help to explain or even partly excuse the perpetrator's behaviour.* It may be that the perpetrator was perceived to be acting out of character – stressed or hitting out because they themselves had been hurt in some way. There are many possibilities under this category. Frequently however there is some delay in considering the area of mitigation of responsibility. In the initial stages of shock, anger and hurt, the victim is focusing more on the negative aspects of the perpetrator's behaviour. Consideration of mitigating circumstances usually requires some time to have elapsed since the incident and emotions to be less raw.
- *Whether the perpetrator has shown any remorse.* Research has indicated that this is influential in determining how easy or difficult the victim will find it to forgive the perpetrator. Obviously the more remorseful the perpetrator is the more likely forgiveness is to occur; however it is not a simple equation, and other factors such as the degree of wrongdoing, the amount of hurt and so on will influence the process significantly.
- *Whether the perpetrator has apologized.* Again research has shown that where perpetrators apologize to victims, forgiveness is more likely to be achieved. Again this will, however, be heavily influenced by the nature of the transgression.

As you can see, making judgements are complex processes, but we mostly do it automatically. We do not sit down with a list of criteria like this and work through each one systematically, weighing each factor against what has happened to us. We are normally ruled by our emotions when we have been wronged, we are hurting and angry and as a result we may not be thinking very logically. We believe ourselves simply to be feeling the hurt, anger and injustice that the other person has inflicted on us. We are generally not aware of having been through any judgemental process relating to the wrong we have experienced. Yet this decision-making process is the way that human beings make sense of the behaviour of others. We all have a store of social knowledge that we have built up over our lives, and we use it when making the judgements that help us to understand the behaviour of others. When we find ourselves thinking or saying such statements as, 'He should not treat me this way, how dare he do that,' we know that we have used this store of information to make a judgement about the way that person has treated us. We know how we expect to be treated, and how we think others should behave. We are all highly practised at doing this and it happens so quickly that we are unaware of the process.

It can be very helpful to explore in detail the decision-making process you have gone through to arrive at some judgement of a wrongdoing where you feel you were a victim. Some people are initially a little reluctant to do this – they do not want to experience the emotions yet again – but going through this process is usually extremely helpful. In beginning to understand where the hurt has come from, and exploring the judgements you have made, you can begin to distance yourself emotionally from what has occurred. This exercise is designed to help you explore the factors that have contributed to your final judgement. You may find it distressing to complete, but this is a valuable exercise. It will help you to begin to explore your feelings about the event in a more systematic way. In my experience from clinical work, writing down your feelings and trying to rate aspects of the event helps you to think more objectively and less emotionally about what has occurred.

EXERCISE

Exploring the wrongdoing

Focus on an event where you felt someone wronged you. Describe in a few sentences for yourself the nature of this event.

_____

_____

_____

_____

_____

_____

1 How bad do you feel what happened to you was?

As bad as I could imagine / Very bad / Bad / Quite bad / A little bad

2 How distressed were you by the wrongdoing?

As distressed as I have ever been / Very distressed /
Fairly distressed / Distressed / A little upset

3 How intentional was the act? Mark the appropriate point on the line.

Totally
premeditated _____ Accidental
(They really
meant to do it)

4 Is this incident part of a typical pattern of behaviour that you have experienced from this person?

Yes / No / Sort of

5 How frequently has she/he/they behaved like this before to you?

Never / Once / Twice / Three times / Frequently

6 How frequently has she/he/they behaved like this before to other people to your knowledge?

Never / Once / Twice / Three times / Frequently

7 How long have you known this person? _____

8 How close did you feel your relationship *was* to this person?

Very close / Close / Friendly / Not very close / Neutral

9 Can you think of any reasons that might help to explain the way the perpetrator behaved towards you? Note them down.

_____

_____

_____

_____

_____

_____

10 Has the perpetrator shown any remorse (sorrow) for what they did?

Yes / No / Sort of

11 How remorseful (sorry) have they been? Mark the appropriate point on the line.

Very
remorseful _____ No remorse

12 Has the perpetrator apologized?

Yes / No / Sort of / Tried to

Once you have completed this exercise you need to spend some time reading back over it as this will help you to understand more precisely why you are feeling the way you do. You may find it useful to put it on one side for a few days and then re-read what you have written. Many people find this helps them begin to distance themselves emotionally from what has happened to them. They have lost some of their anger. They can look at the situation in a slightly more detached way than previously.

Sometimes people tell me that they have shared their responses with someone else and this person has disagreed with some of what they have written. Other people may see something differently from the way that you, the victim, have recorded it. At this stage this is unimportant. Do not be drawn into arguments about the interpretation of events. You are exploring how _you_ feel. You need to record your feelings faithfully. Remember, we all see the world somewhat differently and at this point we are interested in _your_ views. At a later stage you will be more prepared to take on the views of others.

3

The difficulty of forgiving

We are dealing with complex emotions and situations. In this chapter we step back from focusing on the specific wrongdoing and related aspects of non-forgiveness to explore more general issues relating to forgiveness. We explore some of the factors that help us maintain our feelings of hurt and may make it more difficult for us to forgive. It is widely accepted that having a wrong done to you is unfortunate and can be distressing but we tend not to recognize that there are some benefits to being a victim and these will be examined. Finally we look at the costs of non-forgiveness to us personally and the benefits of forgiveness. Hopefully with the help of this section victims will be more motivated to work towards forgiveness, as it will be clear that it is in their best interests to forgive, or at least draw a line under the past. As before, the person who has had a wrong done to them is referred to as the *victim* and the wrongdoer as the *perpetrator*.

The role of other people

If you have completed the preceding exercise you will now better understand the factors that have influenced your judgement in relation to the wrong that has been done to you. You may also be somewhat clearer about your feelings relating to the event. However these processes have not occurred in isolation. No doubt, when the wrong occurred, you discussed what happened with significant others in your life. We know from research in social psychology that these people usually reinforce the victim's judgement about the perceived wrongdoing of the perpetrator. The behaviour of those supporting the victim is an important consideration, as this can be a significant source of escalation of the magnitude of the wrongdoing. This may well have happened to you.

Think about our own behaviour in such an instance. When something unfortunate happens to a friend or colleague, publicly we may sympathize with them, though in private we may feel differently. Perhaps we think they 'had it coming to them', or that they contributed to the problem in some way. Social pressure makes us publicly agree in this case with the victim. We do not want to add to their hurt by disagreeing with them, so we go along with how they describe the situation to us and accept that their feelings are valid in the situation they are in. In terms of psychological learning theory, however, this expression of sympathy reinforces the victim's view that what has happened to them is wrong, especially if that reinforcement comes from a source they see as powerful or 'expert' in some way. The victim's perception of events is thus confirmed. When others are seen to agree with our view of the wrongdoing in this way, we are likely to hold on to our views even more strongly, and be less open to change.

Not everyone may agree with the victim's version of events. However, anyone trying to present a slightly different interpretation may not be well received. It is worth returning to the point about how we each create our own version of reality, our own perception of a situation. Bearing this in mind it can be helpful to listen to others' perception of the situation. They are unlikely to be as emotionally involved as the victim and may provide useful insights. It is better if they are seen to be expressing their own opinion rather than attacking the victim's perception of events – a minor distinction but an extremely important one. The victim may find it valuable to obtain another person's account of the situation. How do they explain what has happened? It is important that the victim is not too defensive and able to listen to other, considered opinions, especially if the person giving them is not particularly emotionally involved. However, it can be some time before most of us are willing or able to listen to other opinions about the wrongdoing. We need to get over our initial shock and feel less upset by the situation. By completing the tasks outlined so far, we should be beginning to reach this position.

So far we have painted a picture where most people, either through conviction or social pressure, or perhaps a bit of both, publicly agree with the victim's interpretation of events. There may be the odd person trying to mediate, presenting what might seem to the victim to be an interpretation that is slightly more positive towards the perpetrator. Psychologists have looked at how people acquire their beliefs and we know from this work that this kind of situation produces behaviour that is fairly difficult to change. Forgiveness is not easily bestowed, since there are many factors to support the status quo.

The benefits of non-forgiveness

While the negative consequences of being a victim are obvious – the hurt feelings, the anger, the upset – there are also some positive features. As we have seen, victims tend to elicit sympathy. They may feel morally superior to the perpetrator. They may have a strong sense of being in the right, of being justifiably angry and hurt, and that they have a right to retaliate. Being a victim may actually endow them with more power than they normally have. Friends may pay them more attention; they may get privileges not otherwise given. People in positions of power may promote their case, as sometimes happens in work situations, where a supervisor or manager provides sympathy and support. They may have power over the perpetrator; this is especially apparent in threatened partnership breakdowns, where one party has transgressed, leaving the other in the role of victim. Sometimes complex power games are played out with the perpetrator, and the victim may relish the power that their partner's transgression has bestowed on them.

On a personal level, non-forgiveness also has the benefit of making the individual feel safe. By not forgiving, the individual is avoiding contact with the perpetrator as much as possible. By forgiving, they re-establish contact and leave themselves open to be maltreated in the future. If someone has treated you badly, they have violated your trust. It is natural to feel that there is nothing to stop them repeating their behaviour on a future occasion. We need and like to receive approval and feelings of goodwill from other people. This need makes us vulnerable, as it gives them power over us. By not forgiving, we are in effect saying that we do not need or want anything from this person and are thus protected from them. By forgiving the perpetrator the victim may be afraid of appearing weak. Forgiving may be seen as backing down, and this may increase the reluctance of the victim to engage with forgiveness. No one likes to be perceived as being weak and we may feel that forgiveness may be seen as weakness. This may be especially true if we have received a lot of support and sympathy from our friends when the wrongdoing occurred. It may be even more difficult to be seen to 'change your mind'. Thus non-forgiveness has a fairly powerful protective function in that it serves to distance the victim from the perpetrator. It also gives them some rights, and perhaps power, over the perpetrator they may not have had previously, and sympathy and support from others in their lives.

The costs of non-forgiveness and the benefits of forgiveness

So far we have come to appreciate the complexity of a situation in which we are hurt. While the victim undoubtedly suffers greatly there are also some advantages, or what psychologists term 'secondary gains', from being a victim. These can be quite powerful, and can decrease the victim's motivation to forgive. It is therefore necessary to look at the costs of non-forgiveness and grudge-holding, to both the individual and their wider social group.

Research on forgiveness indicates that people who are more forgiving experience better psychological health than those who are less forgiving. As we have discussed, human beings are sociable by nature and most of us find things infinitely more comfortable when we are at peace with those in our social world. Being at odds with someone is inherently stressful. We find ourselves continually ruminating about our hurt and perhaps fantasizing about the perpetrator getting their just deserts. We may even scheme around ways of making this occur. Under these conditions it is extremely difficult to move on to new things. The perceived hurt/wrongdoing dominates the present and this continued focusing on what has occurred consumes all the victim's emotional energy. The victim is trapped in an emotional circle of continuing hurt and anger, and this may be accompanied by feelings of impotence towards the perceived perpetrator. They are totally convinced that the perpetrator should be punished in some way, shown up to be the dreadful person they really are. Some sort of retribution should be made to them, the victim, but they do not see how this is ever going to happen. It is thus apparent that such a state is extremely stressful for the individual and the significant others in their lives.

A great deal of research has been undertaken looking at the effects of stress. This has shown that prolonged stress is bad for both our physical and psychological health. Highly stressed individuals are more likely to suffer from headaches due to muscle tension, gastrointestinal problems, skin rashes, dizziness and fatigue. Stress can lead to high blood pressure, which in turn is associated with the development of heart conditions, and also stroke and kidney failure. Such long-term stress is known to affect our immune systems, so we are more susceptible to all sorts of infections. Chronic conditions such as arthritis, colitis, asthma, hypoglycaemia, ulcers and diabetes can be aggravated by chronic stress. The conclusion has to be that unresolved stressful situations, such as those involving non-forgiveness, harm both our physical health and psychological well-being. By not working towards forgiveness, or at least putting the past behind us, we may be significantly increasing our stress levels and so may damage our health. We are certainly reducing our opportunities for happiness in the future.

Forgiveness can therefore be usefully conceptualized as a form of stress reduction. By letting go of the hurt and anger, the victim can put the events behind them and become fully engaged with the present once more. They are also likely to free up some of their emotional energies to engage in new activities and move on with their lives.

The act of forgiving may also reap rewards in terms of improved relationships within our social circle. Holding grudges, showing bitterness towards the perpetrator, and always replaying the wrongdoing may result in the victim gradually losing the sympathy of family and friends. It is a harsh truth that others do get tired of being supportive, of the constant misery and anger. It is assumed that people will eventually 'get over' things and move on. Failure to do so comes to be viewed unsympathetically; it may even be seen as pathological. We have all heard people make comments about how sad it was, what happened to X, but really it is time they got over it, made an effort, stopped sounding like a stuck record, and so on. The sympathy of friends and family tends to be time-limited. If loved ones begin to seek more rewarding company, the victim can become socially isolated, and consequently even more unhappy.

What if forgiveness is not possible?

The human capacity to forgive is actually awe-inspiring. There are countless examples of this through history, from Jewish concentration camp survivors who have no bitterness against their captors, to abandoned or abused children who grow up to be caring individuals and appear to bear no grudges. But what if someone feels that forgiveness is not possible? It may be that they feel the wrong committed against them is too great to forgive. The murder or serious mistreatment of a child are examples of events where those affected frequently say that forgiveness of the perpetrator is impossible. For others it may be their individual personality that makes it more difficult for them to forgive. It may be that the perpetrator has not apologized and has no intention of doing so. The perpetrator may not even agree that any wrong has been done to the victim.

In these instances, where forgiveness seems an unachievable goal, advances can still be made, as we shall see later. A distinction needs to be made here between active non-forgiveness – bearing a grudge, seeking retribution – and more passive non-forgiveness as a statement of belief or philosophy of life relating to the particular events. It is active non-forgiveness that is stressful, with its continued focus on the hurtful events and the perpetrator. It is possible, while not forgiving someone, to put the past behind you and get on with your life, to draw a line under the experience and refuse to allow the perpetrator to continue to make you angry and unhappy. Some of the strategies to help with this will be explored later.

In other instances, the perpetrator is no longer part of the victim's life. They may be separated socially or geographically, or the perpetrator may have died. But forgiveness is still achievable even where there is no longer any contact with the perpetrator. For example, in the course of therapy some people, perhaps through their own experiences as parents come to interpret differently the behaviour of a deceased parent. An increased understanding of why their parent acted as they did may cause them to change their view of the parent. They may move from thinking of the parent as having been harsh and uncaring to seeing them as damaged and unhappy, perhaps due to problems in their own upbringing. In other words, mitigating circumstances are considered retrospectively and may be powerful enough to change perceptions, especially when the direct influence of the parent is no longer a reality. Such forgiveness is worth striving for, as it can bring health benefits. Individuals report feeling more at peace with themselves, being able to put the past behind them and to focus more on the present and the future. They feel happier in themselves and more confident in their ability to cope with the world.

Working towards forgiveness

Working towards forgiveness can be seen as a courageous step. Others generally appreciate the difficulty involved in the process and may well offer support and encouragement, once they are aware that the victim is trying to let go of their hurt and anger and work towards some sort of resolution. However, there may be some initial difficulty if family and friends are still at the stage of providing sympathy to the victim; reiterating the view that what was done was 'unforgivable', yet the victim is beginning to feel it is perhaps time to begin to move on. Some sharing of feelings may be necessary, and it can be difficult. Sometimes victims say that they would like to put the incident behind them, but this is not possible because of the anger or hurt continually being expressed by others close to them. It is sometimes necessary on these occasions to work not just with the victim.

It can obviously help if the perpetrator apologizes, shows remorse and tries to make amends in some way. But forgiveness is still worth striving for even where this is not the case. People who forgive are generally happier and less stressed than those who continue to hold grudges and seek retribution. By focusing on the event and experiencing the related anger and hurt, you are continuing to let the perpetrator affect you. It is a harsh reality for many to accept but by failing to try to come to terms with the perceived wrongdoing and to move on with your life, you are actually escalating the wrong done to you. In addition, you are quite likely to be damaging your own health. The psychological stress associated with non-forgiveness cannot be over-emphasized. By hanging on to this grievance, with its related feelings of anger and injustice, you are still allowing the perpetrator to impact negatively on your daily life. *They are still hurting you and you are allowing it to happen.*

At this point some victims can become angry and resentful towards counsellors and therapists who are trying to convey this message. The therapist is obviously failing to understand the enormity of what has happened to them. No insensitivity is intended, however, the therapist's main aim is to help the victim reduce the stress in their life related to the damaging incident and so be happier in the long run. There are unfortunately no quick, easy solutions. It takes determination and application on the part of the victim to work through the anger and hurt and come to a resolution of whatever kind. But the effort is worthwhile in terms of the benefits to be gained: your achievement will be admired by others, you will be happier working towards forgiveness than settling into a life of grudge-holding and bitterness, and the reduction in stress will have a positive impact on your health.

4

The journey to forgiveness

Although we may accept that achieving forgiveness would be advantageous in terms of improving our health and happiness, it can be difficult to commit to the process. The next step is to carry out a costs/benefits analysis of forgiving the perpetrator. This allows the victim to discover exactly what is involved in the commitment to change their feelings, and to understand the complexity of the process. It can also help them to identify how they feel and explore how much change is actually possible. Every victim's situation will be unique, but the following questions will help to identify the likely areas that need to be explored, and guide the individual through the process.

Costs/benefits analysis

Return to the incident you described in the exercise at the end of Chapter 2 (page 16). It may be helpful to copy your description out again at the beginning of the exercise below or on a separate sheet of paper. It is not essential to focus on the same event, but a deeper understanding of the process is likely to be obtained by following the same event through all the exercises included in this book.

EXERCISE

Costs and benefits of non-forgiveness and forgiveness
Focus on an event where you felt someone wronged you. Describe in a few sentences for yourself the nature of this event.

_____

_____

_____

_____

_____

_____

_____

_____

_____

_____

_____

Next you need to make judgements about various issues related to the wrongdoing. Record them by circling the responses that describe how you currently feel about the wrongdoing, indicating the strength of your feelings about each item that is applicable to your situation. You may wish to expand on your responses – use additional sheets of paper if the issues are complex.

This is not an easy exercise and it may take some time to complete, but it is an important stage of the process of trying to understand the exact nature of your situation. It will allow you to explore your feelings in a systematic way, and people often report that writing down their feelings and opinions in this way removes some of their emotional impact, putting some distance between them and their emotional responses. It can lead to a more objective perception of the situation and you will also have a useful record to reflect on and to help you deepen your understanding. The aim is to help you clarify exactly what the situation means to you, to see what is involved in making changes, and indeed to see whether / how much change is possible for you. I would emphasize again that this can be a difficult and painful exercise. Please be as honest as you can when exploring your feelings.

We begin with the benefits of not forgiving, as this is usually the easiest part to complete. However, it may not be that simple: some things may appear to be both benefits and costs. It is your feelings that are important – go with them. We can all be illogical in our thinking. It is part of being human. So do not be afraid of displaying inconsistent thoughts and feelings. Only by owning them and exploring them can you come to truly understand how you feel about the position you are in.

Benefits of not forgiving

1 I receive sympathy and more attention than I would normally do.

True / False

Main sympathizers (give details):

_____

_____

_____

_____

_____

_____

How important is this to you?

Very important / Important / Unimportant / Unsure

2 I feel morally superior to the perpetrator.

True / False

How important is this to you?

Very important / Important / Unimportant / Unsure

3 I have a strong sense of being in the right, of being justifiably angry and hurt.

True / False

How important is this to you?

Very important / Important / Unimportant / Unsure

4 I feel I have the right to retaliate.

True / False

How important is this to you?

Very important / Important / Unimportant / Unsure

5 I feel that I now have some power over the perpetrator that I did not have previously.

True / False

How important is this to you?

Very important / Important / Unimportant / Unsure

6 List any other perceived advantages emanating from others (e.g. privileges you would not otherwise have, other people looking after your interests or promoting your case).

_____

_____

_____

_____

_____

_____

7 I feel safe, as I can use the situation to avoid or minimize contact with the perpetrator.

True / False

How important is this to you?

Very important / Important / Unimportant / Unsure

8 By not forgiving I can feel strong, and there will be no loss of face on my part.

True / False

How important is this to you?

Very important / Important / Unimportant / Unsure

9 Maintaining a state of non-forgiveness makes me feel stronger.

True / False

How important is this to you?

Very important / Important / Unimportant / Unsure

10 List any other benefits for you.

_____

_____

_____

_____

_____

_____

_____

Costs of not forgiving

1 I feel distressed a lot of the time.

True / False

Put a cross on the line below to indicate the level of distress you feel.

Extremely   No
distressed _____ distress

2 I feel more anxious than I used to in social situations.

True / False

Record your level of anxiety by putting a cross on the line below.

Extremely   No
anxious _____ anxiety

3 I feel very angry about the event.

True / False

Record your level of anger by putting a cross on the line below.

Extremely   No
angry _____ anger

4 I find it difficult to stop thinking about it.

True / False

Rate how much you think about it.

| All the | | Not at |
| time | _____ | all |

5 Thinking about it is stopping me getting on with my life.

True / False

Rate how much it interferes.

| A great | | Not at |
| deal | _____ | all |

6 I am finding it hard to trust people.

True / False

Record your degree of difficulty trusting others.

| Impossible to | | Not a |
| trust | _____ | problem |

7 The whole episode is making me feel ill:

- My sleep is disturbed   True / False
- I am more tired.   True / False
- I am more irritable.   True / False
- I am more easily upset.   True / False
- My appetite is disturbed – either
  eating more (in terms of 'comfort'
  eating) or suffering from loss of
  appetite.   True / False
- I have lost my interest in sex.   True / False

Record the degree to which the event(s) have affected your life.

| Huge | | No |
| effect | _____ | effect |

8 It is disrupting my family/social relationships.

True / False

Record the degree of disruption.

Huge
disruption _____ None

9 People do not interact normally with me. (They may be sorry for you, embarrassed, unsure of what to say, or wary of you in some way.)

True / False

Record the extent to which you think this is happening.

A great   Not at
deal _____ all

10 I run the risk of becoming a bitter person.

True / False

11 List any other effects on you or your family/relationships.

_____

_____

_____

_____

_____

_____

Review your analysis

At this stage, stop and review what you have written. You may want to discuss your responses with a friend or partner. Sometimes onlookers are more aware than you are of the effect the situation is having on your health and psychological well-being. They may suggest additional factors; you need not accept them, but it may be useful to get another person's perspective at this point. One benefit of talking to someone close to you is that this may enable them to understand better exactly what you are going through.

If you don't want to share your feelings with others again this is fine. You are doing this for yourself and you decide what is right for you at any particular time. This is very private, personal material. You may be acknowledging some very harsh truths, which are difficult enough for us to explore on our own, never mind sharing them with someone else. Sometimes people get upset about what they have written, feeling it does not show them in a good light. It is perfectly normal and understandable for you to wish to protect yourself from further hurt. You need to know that you are getting support from others, not criticism. It is very important that you do not feel upset, annoyed or disappointed with yourself for acknowledging that there are benefits to be gained from not forgiving someone. You are being brave exploring your feelings in this way.

A word of caution is necessary for the person you share your feelings with, should you choose to do so. Most victims are not ready at this time to have their views contradicted, and it's not a good idea to try to persuade them out of their perception of events. The victim needs the other person to share in exploring the negative effects that the situation has had on them, and to know if there are any other effects that the person has noticed of which the victim may be unaware.

Although you may have found this a difficult exercise, you should now have a better understanding of the effect that not forgiving is having on you. Look at the costs of not forgiving first. People who complete this are often struck by the effect on them of the costs of not forgiving. Living with unresolved issues is extremely stressful – it may even be making you ill.

Now look at what if any benefits there are in your situation related to non-forgiveness and how important these are to you. How long-term are these benefits likely to be? For most people the benefits are fairly short-term, while the costs are more far-reaching. It is a harsh reality that sooner or later family and friends will move on, and become less sympathetic towards you. As we have seen, the advantages of forgiveness are multiple. You will feel better psychologically and physically, you will stop dwelling on the past and begin to pick up the pieces of your life. Your relationships with others will improve. You will be maximizing your chances of finding happiness in the future.

The difficulty of achieving true forgiveness

After the work you have done in this chapter you should now have a better understanding of the complexity of your feelings about the situation. You are now ready to begin to work towards achieving some degree of forgiveness. People often feel at this point that true forgiveness will never be attainable. Keep reminding yourself that you will never know what is possible unless you give it a try. Think of occasions in the past where you have been surprised at how you coped or what you achieved in a difficult situation. We are all stronger and capable of more than we tend to believe. I am constantly amazed at the capacity of human beings to forgive. People can and do come to terms with dreadful things.

James's wife ran off with his best friend when their son, Michael, was only six months old, leaving the child with him. James brought up Michael on his own, sometimes facing considerable hardship, but always coping. They had a good relationship. He had never heard from Michael's mother. He understood that she had gone to live in Australia with her new partner. When Michael was 22, a relative told him that his mother had returned to live in a neighbouring city. She had not been in contact with him but he decided that he would like to meet her. Privately James was apprehensive about the meeting, but publicly supported Michael, saying he did not have any problem with him trying to make contact with his mother.

Michael met his mother and they began to build a relationship over the next few months. However tragedy struck when Michael was attending a party at his mother's house. There was a fracas involving his mother's partner and another man. Michael intervened to break up the confrontation, and he was fatally stabbed.

James was devastated. For a long time he felt that his life had ended. He was murderously angry with his former wife and her partner, and blamed himself for allowing Michael to contact his mother. Rationally he knew that as an adult Michael was free to do what he wanted, but he still felt very guilty, as if somehow he should have been able to keep his son safe. He even blamed himself for having married Michael's mother in the first place.

Over time, however, he stopped blaming himself. He eventually came to see that hanging on to his anger was not helping anyone – he was hurting himself and driving others away. He came to realize that Michael would not have wanted him to continue through life this way. While he felt that he never came to the point of really forgiving his wife and her partner, gradually his anger lessened and he actually felt some pity for them, knowing how badly it had affected them, and aware that they had to live with their feelings of responsibility for what happened to Michael for ever.

True forgiveness may indeed be difficult to achieve, but everyone can work towards some helpful resolution of their feelings. As long as you continue to feel upset and hurt, you are allowing the perpetrator to exert an influence over you. They are winning, if you like to think of it that way. They have hurt you and are continuing to do so, but you can work towards putting an end to it. In the next chapters we will explore ways of working towards the gift of forgiveness.

PART TWO:
LEARNING TO FORGIVE

5

Addressing the perpetrator
(in virtual reality)

At this point, now you have made a commitment to work towards forgiveness, you need to acknowledge that it may take some time to achieve forgiveness. You have become aware of the complexity of your thoughts and feelings and you need to sort things out in your own mind. You may have been harbouring hurts for a very long time and you cannot be expected to let go of all your negative feelings quickly. Making a commitment to work towards forgiveness is the first step of your journey. No one can insist that you forgive him or her. Forgiveness is a gift that is within your power to bestow on the perpetrator. Yes, we are aware that the gift of forgiveness will also bring many benefits to you, but in fact forgiving someone is often an altruistic act. It involves courage and often enormous generosity. People who have achieved forgiveness commonly talk of it as an enriching and invigorating experience. Their lives have been transformed in a fundamental way. They think differently, are more at peace with themselves and more accepting of others. With these hopefully inspiring thoughts we now begin to explore some of the exercises and techniques that others have found useful in their journey towards forgiveness.

In what follows there is a degree of self-selection. I include a number of different exercises and techniques that individuals have found helpful, in varying degrees, depending on the nature of their circumstances. They vary in terms of how difficult they are to practise and how long they take to implement. We start with the easier ones and progress through to the more difficult. Inevitably, while the focus of the exercise is on achieving forgiveness, there is a significant element of self-exploration involved and this can be enjoyable and rewarding.

Write a letter

When someone has hurt us we tend to spend a lot of time going over in our minds what we would like to say to that person. A lot of our

39

energies are taken up with this. We may wake in the night with an angry dialogue going on in our heads, or be unable to sleep because of it.

Many people find it helpful to put all of this down on paper. I want you to write a letter to the perpetrator. This is not a letter you intend to share with the perpetrator – or at least not at this stage, if ever. I need to stress this point. *You are not writing a letter that you intend to send to the perpetrator.*

The purpose of writing the letter is:

- to allow you to express exactly what your feelings are at this time about what has happened;
- to tell the perpetrator what it has meant to you;
- to clarify to the perpetrator any ways that you think they have misunderstood or misjudged you;
- perhaps to say what you wish had happened;
- to get everything negative about the situation off your chest.

This is a private letter, for you to record all your grievances against the perpetrator and the situation. The aim of the letter is further clarification of your feelings and to allow you to get things 'off your chest'. Writing things down, so that you can go back to them later and reflect on them, gives them an objectivity that they do not have when they are merely thoughts in your head. With the written word we distance ourselves a little from the emotional content and we can begin to look more objectively at what has happened.

Take your time over this, and re-read what you have written. You will probably find yourself returning to it several times, making additions or alterations. You need to ask yourself if this seems a fair account of what has happened from your point of view. Many people find that after a few days the account they end up with is very different from the one they began with. Getting their thoughts down on paper results in them spending less time ruminating about them. For some people it is a very rewarding experience. One woman talked of it as 'drawing a line over the past'.

Somehow I felt as if I had said it all. I had got it all out of my system. I certainly felt less angry and upset. If I am honest, I also saw the situation a little differently. I began to see that perhaps it was not as straightforward as I had first thought. I did not achieve forgiveness but it certainly made me feel better and I could cope better. Forgiveness came much later for me, but the letter writing exercise certainly helped. I still have the letter. I came across it the other day and it was strange to read it now. I can't imagine feeling that way now. I know if something similar happened now I would handle it differently. I would not get so upset.

This woman's experience neatly summarizes the impact that this exercise can have. We all know the satisfaction that comes from 'getting something off your chest' and this letter-writing exercise is a safe way to do this. Initially you may not see the point of writing a letter if you are not going to share it with the perpetrator, but my experience is that it can be a very helpful exercise. It is frequently seen as a useful way to begin to regain some control over your feelings. Indeed for some people there is no possibility of ever sharing their feelings with the perpetrator. The perpetrator may be in a position of power, or they may not be in contact with the perpetrator any longer.

A male client had harboured enormous resentment, bordering on hatred, for his now deceased father, because of the way he had been mistreated while he was growing up. Initially he said he felt very silly writing to someone who was dead, but he persevered. He ended up producing quite a long journal in which he explored his feelings about what had happened to him over the years. He reported this as a cathartic experience, and as a result he felt he was able to put the past behind him once and for all.

I know of a few instances where these letters, or modified versions of them, have been shared with the perpetrator, with mixed results.

Margaret, a grown-up daughter, was feeling very hurt by the way she felt that her mother had always favoured her brother. It had all resurfaced in an incident where Margaret felt that she and her children had been slighted by her mother giving preference to her brother's needs. Margaret had recently had her second child, and she had a long-standing agreement that her mother was to come to look after the baby and her elder child for a week to allow Margaret to accompany her husband on a business trip overseas. Margaret had had a difficult pregnancy and labour and was looking forward to the trip enormously.

A few days before she was due to go, her mother rang to say she was unable to come. Margaret's brother's child-care arrangement had fallen through; he and his wife were attending a conference together in America, the week that Margaret was also due to be away. Years of resentment about the preference shown to her brother surfaced.

After completing the writing exercise, Margaret shared a modified version of the letter with her mother. Initially it caused great ructions within the family, and it was only after her brother intervened, agreeing that there was some justification in Margaret's claims, that some sort of peace was restored. It took a long time for relationships to be fully repaired, and in retrospect Margaret admitted that sharing her feelings in that way had not been very helpful. But at the time she had felt she had no option. Longer term, however, she thought that it had benefited their relationship, as her mother was now more considerate and she appreciated the efforts that her mother made.

One person in a relationship may be ready to be open about their feelings and actions, but this does not mean that the other is. It can be very risky to share your innermost thoughts and feelings with the perpetrator at this stage. You need to understand your feelings and distance yourself from the immediacy of the situation before you are ready to engage with the perpetrator, if indeed you ever need to.

You may find yourself revisiting your letter from time to time and revising the contents as your perception of the situation changes. This can be helpful as it shows you how your feelings are changing – it can be used as a measure of the progress you are making and of just how far you have come on your journey. Everyone needs positive reminders of how we are progressing. It is easy to become discouraged when you are attempting this difficult task, so take every opportunity to reward yourself and to recognize the progress you are making. You may find that the issues that concern you change – some may diminish and others become more important. This is perfectly normal and you simply need to stick with it. You are on a difficult journey but the end will be worth it for you!

In the material that follows, some sections will be more relevant to how you feel than others. I am trying to be inclusive and to cover all the common problems associated with non-forgiveness. If you wish, select the sections that fit with where you currently are on your journey to forgiveness and work only on those. Or you may wish to work through the whole book. Some people have said that although they no longer feel angry, they still find it useful to reflect on how they have dealt with their anger. It can be immensely cheering to recognize that you have already made some progress towards coming to terms with your emotions.

6

Understanding our emotions

Thinking about how we control our feelings raises the issue of how our emotional responses are produced. It is something that we seldom reflect on. Our emotional responses are quick and apparently automatic. We tend to think that their generation has little to do with us. We talk about other people making us angry, or happy or sad. Our language is full of such expressions:

He made me so angry the way he just assumed that I would go along.

She does it on purpose, as she knows that it'll wind me up. She makes me so mad!

Every time he leaves the toilet seat up and he knows it drives me mad. I get so furious with it!

I was feeling really happy and in she came and burst my bubble with her moaning and feeling sorry for herself.

At this point you may well be saying, 'But it's true, other people do wind you up, or make you sad.' This is a very common misperception. Stop and think about where your emotional responses come from. It is of course within your own mind and body. We frequently talk about our emotions as if we have no control over them whatsoever. We are just happy, angry or sad – it simply happens, like a shower of rain washing over us.

We need to recognize that emotions do not simply happen, but rather we are actively involved in producing our own emotional responses. Here we explore the body's automatic reactions to stressful events that upset us emotionally. This will help us to understand further why continuing to be upset may actually be causing physical damage to our bodies, resulting in ill-health, as well as psychological hurt. This understanding will reaffirm us in our wish to work towards forgiveness. It may be quite novel for you to consider non-forgiveness as a source of stress, or stressor, as it is labelled by psychologists. However this is sometimes a very useful way of conceptualizing the hurt or wrong and it may help you focus more on trying to minimize the stress it is causing you.

How the body responds to stress

When we are very stressed, our physiology takes over. This occurs when we are feeling threatened in some way – physically or psychologically, the body makes no distinction. It is a biological response, described as 'fight or flight'. We have no initial control over our emotions. Here our biology takes over. The body has an inbuilt system that is mobilized in response to stress. It causes our initial alarm reaction when something very stressful occurs. It is part of our autonomic nervous system.

The autonomic nervous system consists of nerves that carry messages to and from our glands and visceral organs (heart, stomach, intestines, etc.). It has three main functions. First, it controls the essential body functions, such as heartbeat, breathing, digestion, sweating and sexual arousal. Second, and this is what mainly concerns us here, it plays a central role in regulating our emotions. Have you ever stopped to think why, when you are emotionally upset, you sometimes also get a pounding heart, an upset stomach or a headache? It is because the autonomic nervous system regulates both our emotions and the functioning of our internal organs. When we experience some major stressor, our autonomic nervous system gets thrown out of kilter, resulting in our bodily functions becoming disturbed. However this naturally occurring biological reaction dies down fairly quickly as we adapt to the situation, and bodily functions return to normal.

The third function of the autonomic nervous system controls our motivation. This helps explain why when we are upset we may 'comfort eat' or lose our appetite, become overactive, unable to sit still, or alternatively very tired and lethargic, especially if the stress continues for some time.

We know from work by a Canadian researcher, Hans Seyle (1976), that the body responds in much the same way to any threat, be it physical, such as an infection or a tumour, or psychological, like the feelings associated with being hurt. Whatever the source of the stress the body responds by mobilizing its defences. We become alarmed, and the autonomic nervous system kicks in in the ways I have just described. Our heart rate and blood pressure increase, we perspire and our glands pump additional hormones into the bloodstream, resulting in increases in blood sugar. We are being prepared to resist the stressor, the well-known 'fight or flight' protective response. If we do not, or cannot, resolve the situation in some way and the stress continues – as with cases of failure to forgive – then our bodies become less able to deal with the stress. We are then very likely to become ill and /or psychologically distressed.

As mentioned above, the body's stress reaction system does not distinguish between physical and psychological sources of stress; the reaction is the same. Most of the stress we face in our lives nowadays is psychological, and is frequently ongoing. The physical responses produced by our body are unhelpful and even dangerous to our physical health. Suffering prolonged stress can result in increased blood pressure, digestive disorders, sleep problems, increased blood cholesterol levels and blood clotting factors, thereby increasing the risk of heart attacks. Your immune system is adversely affected and so you become more susceptible to infections such as colds and flu and are less able to fight off infections.

How we generate our emotions

These negative effects of prolonged stress, such as the emotional stress associated with non-forgiveness, should encourage us to begin to explore how we can break the cycle and work towards minimizing our distress. To start with we need to explore how to generate our everyday emotional responses and how we maintain our distress about particular events.

The common perception is that it is the things other people do that cause our response, be it what we do or how we feel. This is not the case. When things happen in the world we observe them, describe them to ourselves, and then crucially we evaluate them. How we then feel and what we do depends on that evaluation. Dr Albert Ellis, an American cognitive behavioural therapist, has eloquently described this process. It is based on the premise that we all create our own perceptions of the world. A simple example will help you to understand the process.

Suppose you are out shopping and you see someone you know

from work coming towards you in the crowd. You are preparing yourself to greet them, but they walk right past and do not acknowledge you. Now, depending on how you feel at that time, you may chuckle to yourself and make a mental note to joke with them about their abstractedness next time you see them. The emotional response you are then experiencing is one of *mild amusement*. However, this is not the only possible interpretation of what has happened. Someone else observing their colleague ignoring them may say to themselves, 'How conceited, imagine ignoring me. I always knew she/he was too big for her/his boots.' Now the emotional response that follows from the same piece of behaviour is one of *anger and irritation* at what has been perceived as a slight. Yet another person may perceive that the person failing to acknowledge them is actively ignoring them. They say to themselves that the person is not talking to them. They may then rack their brain, recalling the last interaction they had with that person, trying to recollect if they could possibly have caused offence in some way. The resulting emotional response in this instance is one of *anxiety*.

The conclusion from this and similar observations is that we all participate in this description and evaluation of things that happen in the world. We all create our own realities, our own personalized interpretation of events. For those who are still sceptical there is a wealth of evidence in social psychology demonstrating that it is very difficult to get observers to agree to any 'objective' definition of events in the real world. This is why eyewitness testimony is notoriously unreliable. When we are interpreting and evaluating events, we are heavily influenced by our mood state, our personality and our beliefs about the world.

The ABC model

Dr Ellis developed a simple labelling system to assist in recalling this process that we use to generate our emotional responses. He calls the event under consideration the 'activating event', and labels it the A. Next we describe the event to ourselves and evaluate it. As this is heavily influenced by our 'beliefs' about the world (as well as our personalities and mood state), he labels this the B. Finally there is an 'emotional and/or behavioural consequence' leading from the activating event (A), and he labels this C. The process whereby we generate our emotional responses can thus be easily conceptualized as an ABC model, as shown in the table below, using the previous example and expanding on it to explore the possible influences of B, our beliefs about the world.

The ABC model of emotional generation

A	B	C
The **activating** event.	You describe and evaluate the event to yourself influenced by your **beliefs** about the world, including personality factors and mood.	The emotional and behavioural **consequences** of A.
Example 1 A colleague walks towards you when you are shopping. You are preparing yourself to greet them but they walk right past and do not acknowledge you.	You are very relaxed and enjoying shopping and in a light-hearted mood. You are also someone who does not worry too much about what other people think of you. Your interpretation is that the person is absentminded and your evaluation of the event is quite positive. (It is amusing.)	You may chuckle to yourself and make a mental note to joke with them about their abstractedness next time you see them. The emotional response you are then experiencing is one of mild amusement.

Example 2

A colleague walks towards you when you are shopping. You are preparing yourself to greet them but they walk right past and do not acknowledge you.	You are hot and tired and feeling irritable. You are not enjoying the shopping trip. You are perhaps someone who is very sensitive to being slighted. Perhaps you do not always feel very confident that colleagues like and value you, yet it is important for you to be liked and valued. Your interpretation of the event is that the person has ignored you on purpose as they do not think you are worth talking to. Your evaluation of the event is negative.	You may say to yourself, 'How conceited, imagine ignoring me. I always knew she was too big for her boots.' The emotional response is one of anger and irritation at what has been perceived as a slight.

Example 3		
A colleague walks towards you when you are shopping. You are preparing yourself to greet them but they walk right past and do not acknowledge you.	You are by nature quite an anxious person and worry a great deal about what people think of you. You are easily hurt by the behaviour of others and worry about causing offence yourself, even unwittingly. Your interpretation of the event is that the colleague is actively ignoring you because you must have offended them in some way in the past. Your evaluation of the event is negative.	You are saying to yourself that the person is not talking to you. You then rack your brain, recalling the last interaction you had with that person, trying to recollect if you could possibly have caused offence in some way. The emotional response is anxiety.

We see from this example that although most people assume that it is A (the activating event) that causes C (the emotional or behavioural consequences), it is actually the effect of B that causes C. Because these analytical processes occur so quickly we are generally not at all aware of them happening. We have to stop and think hard about the process to be able to recognize what we are saying to ourselves in any one situation. When the outcome of our interpretation and evaluation is *neutral* or *positive*, then generally it is not a problem for us. When it is *negative*, however, it will cause us some sort of emotional and/or behavioural upset.

Before we begin to analyse the feelings and responses related to issues around non-forgiveness, it will be helpful to spend some time recognizing the response patterns with less emotive material. We can begin by trying to isolate the A (activating event), B (beliefs) and C (consequences), in the following examples. One useful technique is to try to isolate what you are saying to yourself about the particular situation. We all have 'conversations' in our heads, and what we need to know is how what we are saying to ourselves results in us experiencing and expressing the emotions that we have. The difficulty is in recognizing what we are saying to ourselves as we do it so automatically. It can help to write down what has happened. Start with the A, then the C. Give yourself time to go over in your mind what you were telling yourself about A and how you evaluated it. This allows you to explore the effect that your belief system, mood and so on (the B) is having on the judgements you make about situations.

Suzanne is 45 years old and single, and works in an office. She is an only child. Until she was 30, she lived at home with her parents. When her parents retired they sold up the family home and went to live in Spain, and Suzanne had to find somewhere else to live. She lived in a variety of lodgings and rented flats until five years ago when she finally managed to buy a small flat of her own. However, her parents recently returned from living abroad as her mother has been ill. They have bought a nice bungalow near her flat, but now obviously assume Suzanne will give up her flat and move in with them to help look after her mother. Suzanne is tearful and upset, but very unsure of what she feels. She has always done what her parents have told her to do. They are offering her a lovely home that will be hers when they die and she can't understand why she is so upset with her parents, and so ungrateful.

'Dad said the other night, "I don't know how you can stand that poky flat – no views and the walls are paper-thin. It's not worth the money you paid for it." I felt so upset, I couldn't say anything at all. It is a small flat but I have made it nice. He doesn't see that, but that's what he is like. I was quite snappy with him and it is really ungrateful of me when he only wants what's best for me. Sometimes I think I am going off my head. I just don't understand why I feel this way.'

The A (activating event) here was her father's comments about the flat. The C (emotional or behavioural consequence) was Suzanne's feelings of being upset, her 'snapping' at her father and finally her feeling of being ungrateful. Suzanne herself was puzzled by the way she was behaving. She said that her father's comment was typical of him and she could not really understand why she was getting so upset by it. Analysis of what she was telling herself about the A (her father's remarks) proved to be very insightful. Suzanne's commentary on the situation was along the following lines.

How dare he criticize my home? He went off to Spain without a thought for me. He didn't care where I lived. I have paid for this flat myself; he has given me nothing, even although he could have afforded to help me. He never mentioned money for me when he went to Spain; he wanted to make sure that he had enough money for a nice life. He only wants me when it suits him. I really resented him for doing that. He should not have done it. He would not have done it if he really cared for me.

Suzanne was very disturbed by these thoughts, saying that they showed what a nasty person she was underneath and how ungrateful she was. She was a bad daughter. This was her B, her beliefs about what 'good' people felt and how 'good' daughters behaved. She was using these to judge her own thoughts and behaviour. These thoughts were making her feel very guilty. She was telling herself that 'good' daughters did not feel that way, that her parents meant well and that she was a nasty person. Other people would be grateful for what she was being offered.

She had never allowed herself to admit to feeling resentful towards her parents for going abroad and forcing her to leave home. Everyone had assumed that it was what she wanted, and she had gone along with it. Looking back, she could recognize that she held a grudge against her father in particular, as he was the one that made all the decisions in the family. Over time she had simply learnt to accept the situation but she had not analysed her feelings. The return of her parents and their request that she move in with them had reactivated the grudge that she held towards her father.

This case was complicated, as Suzanne was not very good at exploring her feelings or recognizing exactly what she felt at times. She did say, however, that finally coming clean about what she felt was good. It was like a weight coming off her shoulders.

EXERCISE

Think about particular things that have happened recently that have upset you. Do not focus on major events at this stage. This is a first step in the learning process. Now try to complete the A, B and C for each of the following situations.

1 Think about a recent situation where you were *angry*.

A: activating event *What happened.*	B: beliefs about A and evaluations of A *How you described it to yourself and how you evaluated it.*	C: emotional and/or behavioural consequences *What you felt and what you did.*
		Anger.

2 Think about a recent situation where you were *sad*.

A: activating event	B: beliefs about A and evaluations of A	C: emotional and/or behavioural consequences
		Sadness.

3 Think about a recent situation where you felt *guilty*.

A: activating event	B: beliefs about A and evaluations of A	C: emotional and/or behavioural consequences
		Guilty.

You may find it helpful to carry out this exercise several times, as it will help you to begin to recognize the sort of self-talk that you typically have at the B stage. As mentioned earlier, this self-talk happens so automatically that we are usually unaware of it. We do actually go through a process of describing and evaluating events prior to responding to them. You may see some patterns emerging in terms of how the content of your self-talk relates to the emotions you then experience. With practice you will start to see how your distress in particular situations arises. You will become aware of how you evaluate situations, and what it is you are saying to yourself that fuels your feelings.

7

The process of changing our feelings

The link between what we tell ourselves about what has happened and how we feel about it, can be quite difficult for people to really come to understand. It is by no means obvious to us that our feelings are mainly caused by the way that we think. However, generally we do believe that everything has a cause. Things do not simply just happen, something or someone causes them. Therefore this must also be the case for our feelings.

For the examples and from your own work so far, you will have amassed considerable evidence confirming that this is indeed the case. Different people respond to the same event in different ways depending on how they describe and evaluate the situation to themselves. You may see things differently from your friends, depending on how you are feeling at a particular time, the importance of the situation to you and what you believe about the situation (your B). From the understanding of the way that describing and evaluating events leads individuals to feel differently about what appears to be the same situation, you will be aware of how we create our own emotional responses. All of this preparatory work allows us to begin to address the ways in which we can change our feelings.

It must again be stressed that this is not an easy process. It requires much effort to replace our old highly-practised ways of thinking with new, more adaptive thought processes so that we can begin to feel better and move on with our lives. Always remember that you are doing this to improve your chances of happiness and to give yourself peace of mind. Every day that you continue feeling hurt, bitter, angry, afraid, you are allowing the perpetrator to have power over you. You are allowing them to continue hurting you.

The power of the perpetrator

Of the many reasons for trying to achieve forgiveness I find that the one people find most persuasive is the power argument. The understanding that the perpetrator is still wielding their power over them, causing them unhappiness, generally provides the motivation that people need. This is the bottom line for victims who are struggling to achieve some resolution of their feelings towards the perpetrator. One young woman who had suffered sexual abuse put it this way:

> For years I lived in fear of him. He occupied virtually all my waking thoughts. It was always at the back of my mind. I even dreamt about it. Even when it stopped he still continued to haunt me. I was living far away from him but psychologically the hurt was still there. I carried it all in my head. I thought that if he was punished this would help, but even after he was imprisoned it did not go away. Being helped to see that the way I thought about him and what had happened was causing me problems, and that I had the power to change this, transformed my life. I realized that I could not change the past but I could draw a line under it, and work towards thinking differently about it. It is not always easy but when things get tough I say to myself, 'That b— ruined 12 years of your life. Are you going to let him ruin the rest of it?' This thought alone keeps me going. He had power over me for long enough.

This woman was aiming not to forgive the man who had abused her, but simply to stop being upset by what had happened. She wanted to put it all behind her. Indeed if you asked her if she would or could ever forgive the man, the answer would be no. However, as she worked through her feelings and came to understand herself better she found that her anger and hatred towards him became less. While she felt she could never forgive him, she came to feel sorry for him and to see him as a seriously damaged person who was himself incapable of ever being happy. She lost all her feelings of bitterness. She now talked about it as having been very, very sad, and even commented that it had made her what she was and had helped her understand what other people go through. Psychologically she had taken the first steps on the journey to forgiveness and felt much better in herself as a result.

Demanding an apology

This realization that *we cannot change the past* seems very obvious. Yet we may spend a lot of time dwelling on past hurts and injustices, asserting both to ourselves and others that something should not have happened, it was not fair and so on. This does not change anything – rather it ensures that we remain upset. In the context of the ABC model we explored earlier, the A (activating event) is the wrong that occurred in the past, the C (consequence) is our continued emotional distress, and the B (belief system) is our thought that it should not have happened, it is unfair. Our resultant anger and distress are easy to comprehend in this situation. At this point I hear people despair and say, 'But that is the way it is, I am always going to feel this way.' Sometimes this is qualified by, 'I will not get over this until they apologize to me, or until they get what's coming to them.' However, as we saw above, the perpetrator being punished for their wrongdoing does not necessarily make the victim feel any better.

Even if it was guaranteed that we would feel better after an apology, we do not have the power (or I would argue the right) to insist that other people do as we demand. People say things like, 'But they owe me an apology,' 'They must put things right,' 'It isn't fair that they treat me this way and they must not be allowed to do it,' and so on. Here we need to remember what we discussed earlier about how we all tend to see the world differently. *You* may feel that the person treated you very badly, but *they* may not agree with your interpretation of events, and may not feel that an apology is necessary. Even if you are 100 per cent certain that you are owed an apology, you cannot force the other person to apologize and make amends.

Fifteen-year-old Adam was being given a hard time by a couple of lads at school. They were teasing him, and on one recent occasion had taken his homework from him and copied it for themselves. The teacher had not picked up the similarities and the two lads were taunting him about getting him to do all their homework this way.

Adam mentioned this to his aunt, who was visiting over the holidays, and asked her not to repeat it to anyone else. He said he would deal with the situation by handing his work in early and avoiding the two lads as much as possible. She, however, was too concerned to be able to keep quiet about it and told Adam's parents, who contacted the school. A huge fuss ensued, with Adam being interviewed and the two boys eventually being suspended from school for a short time.

Adam was furiously angry with his aunt and said he would never forgive her. He felt he had received unwanted attention at school over something he was perfectly able to cope with himself. He felt that she had violated his trust. Previously he had been very close to his aunt and had felt that she was someone he could confide in. Once his initial anger towards her began to wear off, he recognized that he also felt sad because he had lost his closeness to her. But he insisted that he would never forgive her. Not only had he been betrayed by someone he valued and trusted, he also felt he had been treated like a child, as someone who was incapable of dealing with his own problems – difficult enough for most 15-year-olds to handle. This was his view of events.

From his aunt's perspective, she felt that she had behaved in Adam's best interests and she was sure that he would understand this. She knew that she had a good relationship with him and felt that he trusted her to do what was ultimately best for him. She felt that she had no choice but to tell Adam's parents about the situation. She couldn't have lived with herself if anything else had happened or the situation had become worse and she had done nothing. As Adam raged at her she came to judge him as being unreasonable and increasingly began to feel that *he* should apologize to *her* for the things he was saying and the way he was behaving towards her. Things became much worse with both parties feeling hurt and betrayed and demanding that the other apologize.

We can see how easy it is for both parties to end up feeling that they deserve an apology from the other. Both parties go along thinking that they will never forgive the other and that the other person must offer an apology before they can be forgiven. Both parties are hurt and upset and making demands of each other for apologies or other forms of retribution.

Freedom of choice

However, *we all have freedom of choice in our lives and we cannot demand that other people behave the way we want them to.* We object when other people make demands on us and we have no right to make demands on them. At best we can request and negotiate with others. There may be social and economic constraints that limit our choices, but we can still make choices. This issue can sometimes be contentious. We often claim to have had no choice in a particular situation, but generally what we really mean is that any other action would have been too costly.

A middle-aged woman, Lesley, came to see me to try to understand what was preventing her from leaving an extremely unsatisfactory relationship. She had been married for 27 years and had three grown-up children. Throughout the marriage her husband had been physically and emotionally abusive to her, but never to the children. He had provided well for his family financially although he had never been very involved with the children. She had stayed with him for their sake, as she felt that she could not have cared for them adequately on her own. Throughout the bad times, she consoled herself with the knowledge that when the children left home she would leave her husband and make a new life for herself. When I met Lesley, her youngest child had left home the previous year. She had a secure job, and an aunt had recently died and left her a flat, which she was currently letting but which would provide a suitable home for her. She was very distressed and wanted desperately to know why she was unable to leave, as this had been her goal for years.

For several months Lesley worked hard at understanding her feelings, and identified some of the difficulties she was experiencing. These related mainly to her low self-esteem and related fears of being able to survive on her own. She also worried about how relatives and friends would react to her leaving. After a lot of thought she was adamant that she was leaving and set about putting her affairs in order to prepare for the separation. We agreed to meet again in a month, during which time she was going to be very busy with the move and everything it entailed.

About two weeks later Lesley phoned, very distressed. She was furiously angry, almost incoherent with rage. Her husband had suffered a fairly massive stroke the previous week and was unlikely to make a full recovery. It seemed that he was going to require some level of caring support for the rest of his life. She felt totally trapped. 'You won't believe what that b— has done now. Just as I was leaving him, going to get myself a bit of life, he does this. That's just typical! Now I have to care for him for the rest of my days. I will never forgive him.'

Once Lesley had got over her initial shock, we were able to explore this new situation more calmly. Of course the situation had changed with her husband's incapacity, but she still had a choice. She could still choose to leave him. After setting the benefits of leaving him against the costs, which mainly centred around squaring it with her own conscience and the opinions of her family and friends, she decided that the costs were too great. The crucial thing was that after weighing up the costs and benefits she made a *choice* to stay. She no longer felt trapped into it. She realized that she could have left but that she would not have lived happily with herself had she done so. Once this was resolved she was able to view the facts more dispassionately and make constructive plans to enable her to cope with the altered situation. She ceased to feel bitter. She accepted that of course he had not done it on purpose, and indeed she began to feel some sympathy for him. Some element of forgiveness was apparent. She even commented that although he had been a wicked devil towards her when he was younger, even on her worst days she would not have wished his illness upon him.

This example demonstrates vividly that we do have freedom of choice in virtually all situations. It is simply that sometimes the costs of this freedom are too high for us to live easily with them. However, if we are aware of this we may feel differently about the situations we are in. We are less likely to feel trapped. Knowing that *we* have made a choice, even though the options may be far from ideal, means that we cannot blame anyone else for making us do certain things. We cannot demand that other people do the things we want, and others cannot make such demands on us, although sometimes they may try very hard to do just this.

Recognition that change is necessary

We accept that we all have freedom of choice in our lives and that we cannot demand that other people behave the way we want them to. This leads to the conclusion that the only things we can change are our own behaviour and the choices we make. We can choose to think and behave differently, if we want to enough. If you have consciously completed the earlier exercises and really thought about them you will now be aware that holding on to the hurt and anger towards the person who wronged you is not in your best interests. You can see why you need to change how you feel. At this point we return to the ABC model, and add to it.

Probably the best way to do this is to take you through an example.

Elizabeth was a 23-year-old teacher who had been engaged for two years. John, her fiancé, was a lawyer and slightly older than her. They had gone to the same school and university and knew each other well, having been childhood sweethearts. They were planning a big wedding in May. At Easter Elizabeth's older sister, Sarah, returned from Australia, where she lived, for an extended holiday so that she could participate in the wedding preparations, and she was to be a bridesmaid. To cut a long story short, Sarah and John fell for each other. Two weeks before the wedding, they told Elizabeth and the rest of the family and the wedding was cancelled. Sarah and John went abroad and were married. Elizabeth was adamant that she would never forgive them. Since that time there had been no contact between them and Elizabeth, although Elizabeth's parents had kept in touch. As Sarah and John lived at the other end of the country it had not been difficult for Elizabeth to avoid all contact.

The current crisis had arisen as John's firm had promoted him and this involved returning to his home town. He and Sarah had recently had a baby and Elizabeth's parents were anxious for the rift to be healed. Elizabeth was under a lot of pressure from her parents to make it up with her sister and brother-in-law. Christmas was looming and her mother wanted all her family to be there. She was not prepared to exclude Sarah and John and her first grandchild, as Elizabeth wanted. Elizabeth felt very angry and hurt, and the intensity of her earlier feelings towards Sarah and John seemed to have returned.

To understand the situation we need to look at what Elizabeth was saying to herself about the situation. This means identifying the self-talk that was going on in her mind at the time. As discussed earlier, it can be difficult for us to realize that we are doing this, as self-talk occurs automatically and we do not think about it. This is where the B of the model comes from. Our beliefs, attitudes, personality and mood all affect how we come to describe a particular situation and evaluate it. It is what we are telling ourselves about it. This then influences our understanding of the situation and largely determines how we behave.

Elizabeth perceived that her mother had in fact forgiven Sarah and John. This can be taken as the starting point of our analysis, the activating event.

A: My mother has forgiven Sarah and John.

After some thought, Elizabeth was able to identify what she was telling herself about this event. These thoughts constitute her B.

B: (*These thoughts were all initially about her mother.*)
How dare she?
It is not fair; I am the one who suffered in all this.
She shouldn't do it.
She doesn't really care about me; Sarah has always been her favourite.

These thoughts, as well as making Elizabeth feel angry and upset, were resulting in her absolutely refusing to contemplate any forgiveness of Sarah and John. This then was the *consequence* of her thoughts. For her it was an issue of her mother choosing between her daughters. She was on the verge of telling her mother this.

C: Refusal to have anything to do with Sarah and John.

Underneath this level of distress there remained all the hurt related to the initial event of her cancelled marriage and her sister 'stealing' her boyfriend, as she put it. In many ways this was still the core of her distress. Although three years had passed she had not really adjusted to this. She tried not to think about it and to pretend that it had not happened. When asked if she was successful at doing this she became quite distressed, and admitted how upset she still was. She felt unable to trust any man after what had happened to her and that she would never have another long-term relationship. It was apparent that she mostly blamed her sister. She seemed to feel that men were easy to manipulate and that her sister had somehow gone about enticing John away from her. She said that she now hated her sister and would never forgive her.

As this early hurt was at the core of Elizabeth's distress it was necessary to explore whether she could come to view this event differently, be less distressed by it and even come to forgive her sister. This produced the following ABC.

A: My boyfriend was 'stolen' by my sister.
B: How dare she?
It wasn't fair, it shouldn't have happened.
She went out of her way to get him and she shouldn't have.
She resented the fact that I was getting married first.
Before this she had always been the one to do everything first.
She always seemed better than me.
I looked up to her and loved her and this is how she treated me.
She obviously did not care for me, that she could even think about doing what she did.
She has ruined my life.
C: Hatred of her sister and failure to even contemplate forgiving her.
Blocking her sister out of her thoughts as far as she possibly can and refusing to have any contact.

However, Elizabeth's strategies at C were not really successful, as she was unhappy and had difficulties in relationships with men. She was unable to trust men and could not foresee ever having another long-term relationship.

Elizabeth could see that she was still very unhappy about the situation and she appeared to truly believe that her sister had ruined her chances of future happiness. She did want to feel better about the situation but she could not imagine ever achieving it. She would love to think that she was the type of person who could forgive and move on, but she did not think she was that generous. She said very despairingly, 'I don't think I have it in me.'

This is where the process of change starts: when a person who has some understanding of what they are currently thinking about a situation is unhappy about how they feel and how it is making them behave. As we have seen, there is no one correct reading of a situation; everyone will perceive a situation slightly differently. The first step here, then, was to get Elizabeth to look at *what else* she could be telling herself about the situation that occurred at A.

Evaluating your self-talk

Some people find it useful to work backwards from the C, the consequence. It was clear that Elizabeth would like to put the whole event behind her, to pick up the threads of her relationship with her sister and brother-in-law and be an aunt to the new baby, but she could not see how this could ever occur. She had a fanciful notion that if only she could meet someone and get married, then it might be possible to be in contact with Sarah and John as she would then be on, as she saw it, 'a level plain with them'. As she was not in a long-term relationship she felt this made it even harder for her. Using the example of Elizabeth's current C will make the process clear.

C: Hatred of her sister and failure to even contemplate forgiving her.
   Blocking her sister out of her thoughts as far as she possibly can and refusing to have any contact.

Elizabeth's self-talk (B) is resulting in her being distressed and unable to have contact (C).

B: belief system	C: consequences
How dare she? It wasn't fair, it shouldn't have happened. She went out of her way to get him and she shouldn't have. She resented the fact that I was getting married first. Before this she had always been the one to do everything first. She always seemed better than me. I looked up to her and loved her and this is how she treated me. She obviously did not care for me that she could even think about doing what she did. She has ruined my life.	Hatred of her sister and failure to even contemplate forgiving her. Blocking her sister out of her thoughts as far as she possibly can and refusing to have any contact. Feeling inferior to her sister, as she is not in a long-term relationship.

To change how she feels it is necessary for Elizabeth to change her self-talk. She has made it clear that she would like to feel, if not happy about, then more accepting of the situation, and to be able to contemplate having some contact with her sister and brother-in-law. This is her new consequence (C). Elizabeth needs to consider what she would have to be saying to herself to achieve her new C. This stage of the process usually involves a lot of thought and heart-searching, and later we explore some of the techniques that you can use to help you achieve this. For clarity at this stage we simply add the new self-talk to the table, addressing where possible each item in the previous self-talk.

Belief system (B) that maintained the distress	New belief system required to positively change feelings and behaviour
How dare she? It wasn't fair, it shouldn't have happened.	I can't control what other people do. Life is often unfair and there is nothing I can do about it.
She went out of her way to get him and she shouldn't have.	People don't choose whom to fall in love with, it just happens. It takes two people to make a relationship. I have been unfair in simply blaming my sister.
She resented the fact that I was getting married first.	I have no evidence for this, she seemed happy for me before all this happened.
Before this she had always been the one to do everything first.	On reflection this is untrue, therefore I must stop telling myself this.

She always seemed better than me.	I have always thought this because she is my big sister, but actually I did better at school than her and in my career. There is no evidence for this and it is my problem if I think her better than me. Stop thinking this way as it is unhelpful. Better to think we are both different people with different talents and interests and try not to judge either her or myself.
I looked up to her and loved her and this is how she treated me.	Feeling sorry for myself. She was distressed by what happened. She did not want to hurt me. It was not intended.
She obviously did not care for me that she could even think about doing what she did.	Not true. She did not want to do it. She was upset about it, they both were. Stop thinking like this, it does not help.
She has ruined my life.	Simply not true. I have enjoyed some things since it happened. I have been promoted, bought a new flat, been on holidays and the like. Others can only ruin your life if you choose to let them.

What we are doing here is getting Elizabeth to evaluate her self-talk to see if what she has busily been telling herself is actually true. She has gone through the list of items she had written down at B and asked herself the questions, 'Where is the evidence for this belief? Is it reasonable to think this?' Her answers have been very enlightening. It seems that she has not always been thinking very logically.

She had failed to acknowledge to herself that what had happened had also really upset both Sarah and John. They had not set out with the aim of hurting her. The attraction had simply happened and had been too strong for either of them to ignore. She acknowledged that she had in some ways over-reacted by believing that her life was ruined. It was difficult for her to accept that other people can affect you in this way only if you choose to let it happen. You have the power to stop it.

This step of ultimately accepting responsibility for your own life is one that most of us find difficult. It is much easier and more comforting to continue to blame others for our misfortunes and unhappiness. Others may be instrumental in initially causing our troubles but if we choose to do nothing about it and continue to be upset, then that is down to us. We are responsible for maintaining our own distress. We need to come to terms with this if we are to progress and achieve more satisfactory resolutions of our problems.

Changing your self-talk

Elizabeth then had the difficult task of giving up much of her self-talk. She needed to be very clear about what she was going to say to herself instead, when the topic was alluded to or when she was reminded of it and started to brood. Here it is useful to have a few short ideas or phrases to rehearse that will help you break the unhelpful negative self-talk cycle that you have developed. For Elizabeth this became, 'Neither of them intended this to happen. They did not mean to hurt me. It is better to have found out before we were married.' She wrote this on two cards, one of which she carried in her handbag, so it was always with her, and the other was on her bedside table, as she often got upset last thing at night or first thing in the morning. These 'cue cards' then acted as prompts, when she started with her unhelpful self-talk, to assist her to break the negative cycle.

For Elizabeth then, it is now possible to outline a more positive ABC, which is not going to cause her so much distress and even begins to open the possibility of reconciliation with her sister. This is as follows:

A: My boyfriend was 'stolen' by my sister (same thought as previously).

New B: Not true. They fell in love. Neither of them intended this to happen. They did not mean to hurt me. It is better to have found out before we were married.

C: She still felt sad that it had happened but was much more philosophical about it, accepting that these things happen and that it was better to have found out before the wedding. It was no judgement on her as a person.

Working on this problem also had a knock-on effect on her first problem, her first ABC – her distress at feeling that her mother had forgiven Sarah and John. When this was revisited she found that her views had changed and her worries were somewhat different. Again the old and new elements of her self-talk are shown side by side to allow for easy comparison. We still have the same A, namely, 'My mother has forgiven Sarah and John.'

Belief system (B) that maintained the distress	New belief system that has led to a positive change feelings and behaviour about the A
How dare she?	I have no control what other people think or do. It is natural that she should want to be close to all of her family. She wants to be the peacekeeper and always has done this.
It is not fair; I am the one who suffered in all this.	The world is not a fair place. My mother did actually suffer as well. The whole situation did make her sad and I actually punished her as well. I said nasty things and then I shut her out of my life for a long time as if it were her fault. (Elizabeth felt considerable guilt about this.)

She shouldn't do it.	I can see why she is doing it and I suppose she is right to try, especially with a new baby on the scene. I know I will enjoy being an aunt.
She doesn't really care about me; Sarah has always been her favourite.	Not true. I have no evidence for this. She has always tried to be fair.

From Elizabeth's new beliefs about her situation it is apparent that she felt differently about it. She acknowledged that she had not treated her mother very well in the past and that she had made unfounded claims about her mother favouring her sister and not caring for her. Indeed the guilt she felt about her treatment of her mother made her feel she owed it to her to make it up to her in some way. She knew that agreeing to see her sister and brother-in-law would make her mother happy and she began to consider this seriously. She had moved a long way from her initial position of wanting to force her mother to choose between her daughters and absolutely refusing to contemplate any forgiveness of Sarah and John.

After about three months, Elizabeth went one step further and did indeed make contact with her sister, initially by telephone and then in a face-to-face meeting. She was looking forward to Christmas with all the family being present. She still had a lingering sadness about it all and that will probably always remain. Her relationship with her sister had changed and she felt that they would never again be really close, but as I pointed out to her that could well have happened when her sister married anyway. Her relationship with John was not as difficult as she had imagined it would be, as he had changed in the intervening years and she felt they no longer had so much in common. The baby made things easier for all of them. Elizabeth was still using her cue or prompt cards, including a few new ones, to help her cope, but she felt that she had forgiven Sarah and John and was beginning to put it behind her. A close friend, whose opinion she valued, had applauded her attempts to become reconciled with all her family, telling her that it was a brave and generous act. This had helped her feel even better about herself and determined to try harder.

Changing your habitual thoughts, even when you have committed yourself, is not easily achieved, simply because you have believed the distressing messages for so long. Cards with the new self-talk prompts are one way of helping you cope. These are especially helpful on bad days when it is difficult to be positive and we all get these from time to time. Seeing something written down somehow gives it more authority. I have heard Dr Albert Ellis, who initially developed many of these techniques and applied them to other problems, sum up the problems of changing our thoughts very aptly: 'We are all highly efficient practitioners of dribble.' By this he means that we all spend a lot of time telling ourselves unhelpful things until we truly come to believe them. It may be about how useless we are, or how awful we are compared to other people, or about some other defect that we perceive ourselves to have. We come to believe it because we repeat it to ourselves so often.

Taking our own good advice

One way we can help ourselves to develop a more helpful and less harsh interpretation of a situation that has upset us is to distance ourselves from it.

Write down a short description of a distressing situation. Here you may wish to use the event you detailed in Chapter 2. Then read it as if it were something that happened to one of your friends. Try to imagine your friend telling you about it. It may help to read it out aloud. Now think about the advice you would give to your friend. You may want to write this down as well, as that will help you to really think about it.

Generally we find that people are pretty good at giving advice to their friends but that they tend not to apply the same advice to themselves. For some reason we tend to judge ourselves more harshly than we do our friends. We are, if you like, good advice-givers but not so good at taking our own advice. We find excuses for our friends' behaviour but a lot of the time we do not do this for ourselves. We judge ourselves more harshly and we tend to focus more on our failings than our strengths.

Undertaking this exercise frequently is a good starting-point to begin the process of modifying your unhelpful self-talk and creating more positive messages that will help you to feel better and attempt change. It may be helpful to share what you are doing with a trusted friend, someone whose opinion you value, and really listen to the good advice they give you.

Judging ourselves and others

The discussion of Elizabeth and her self-talk raises some very fundamental issues about the way we think about ourselves and others. We can seem to become obsessed with judging both ourselves and others. Praise and positive judgements of others or ourselves is generally unproblematic; it is the negative judgements we continually make that cause problems. Here I am suggesting that if we all made serious attempts to be non-judgemental it would be better for all of us. I do not mean that we have to approve of everything that everyone does all the time; rather we need to make a distinction between the person and how he or she behaves. We human beings have a lot going for us; we are all capable of behaving in 'good', desirable ways and fundamentally the human race is not bad or evil in some way. I accept that we can all behave badly on occasions, sometimes very badly, but that does not make us bad people, only people who have made a mistake. It does not mean that we are condemned to be bad for ever. We can all change if we want to sufficiently.

Our choice of language frequently makes the problem worse. We do not always say exactly what we mean. The mother who scolds her child by saying, 'You are a bad little boy,' does not really mean that her child is bad, rather she means that her child has behaved badly, in a way that she finds unacceptable in a particular situation. However, young children tend to take language literally and the child may learn that he is a bad person and therefore less lovable. In this way we internalize judgements that other people make about us and we come to make them of ourselves. We tell ourselves that we are 'bad' when we do certain things or think certain thoughts, or that we are 'failures' when all we have done is failed one little examination or not got one particular job. In this way we learn to globally rate ourselves, and this is unhelpful as it lowers our self-esteem. We are more likely to feel bad about ourselves and if this occurs often enough we may get depressed.

A more helpful philosophical stance is to see that human beings

72

are fallible. Human nature means that you will make mistakes in the course of your life. There is ample evidence around you to convince yourself of this. Accepting that it is part of human nature to fail from time to time serves to stop us from blaming ourselves too much when we actually do make mistakes. What usually happens is that we make a great song and dance about our mistake and blow it up out of all proportion, getting ourselves very distressed in the process. As time passes, if we are lucky, we begin to regain some sense of proportion, and then we cope with the situation. (In the meantime we may have done quite a lot of damage both to ourselves and to others.) Even a day can make a huge difference. When something bad happens, if we sleep on it, almost invariably we do not feel quite so strongly about it the next day. Nothing has changed other than we have regained some sense of proportion.

So it is better for our psychological well-being if we can accept that we are bound to make mistakes from time to time, and stop crucifying ourselves when we do so. We need to learn to be more philosophical, to shrug our shoulders and get on with life. In this way we will use our energies more constructively than if we are always complaining about our misfortunes.

What we need to remember is that this is also true of other people: they too will make mistakes simply because they are human. This may help us to stop taking the mistakes of others too personally. It can be very useful to remember this when discussing forgiveness.

Becoming more accepting

The final, general point that needs to be explored in relation to Elizabeth's belief system, but which applies to us all, is to do with our beliefs about the fairness of the world. I am sure we would all agree that it would be preferable if the world were a fair and just place. However, all the evidence suggests that this is far from the truth. Bad things happen to good people who have never done anyone any harm – illnesses, accidents, starvation, natural disasters. The world is anything but a fair and just place. Yet despite all the evidence, most of us still claim that it should be fair when it comes to our own personal business. Bad things should not happen to *us*. Elizabeth claimed that losing her fiancé should not have happened, it was unfair. If we can accept that the world is an unfair place, we may stop being so surprised and upset when apparently unfair things happen to us. I am not saying that we will stop getting upset at all, but we can be less distressed and able to get our feelings under control more easily. Our energies can then be put to better use instead of being tied up with being upset about things we cannot change.

You may not think so at first reading, but these ideas are all very logical and borne out by the evidence around us, if we choose to see it. The aim overall is to help us to become more accepting of ourselves, and less judgemental. We should not expect perfection of ourselves all the time, but accept ourselves as fallible human beings who will fail from time to time but who are no less valuable because of it. We have to learn to like ourselves, and accept ourselves and others for what we are.

Identifying and changing your feelings

We have covered a lot of material in this chapter and some quite difficult ideas. However the basic process is not complicated. All you need to do is systematically apply yourself to the steps described, to explore your current belief system and to begin to look at how this can be changed, and this will allow you to feel better about your situation. As with Elizabeth, you can then begin your journey towards a more helpful resolution of your feelings.

You have several options here: either continue with the situation that you outlined in Chapter 2, or work on one of your scenarios from Chapter 6. What I am endeavouring to do is to teach you a method, a system of getting at what you are thinking so that you can come to understand your feelings and how they come about. Having done this it becomes possible to work at changing them, as we have seen. You will become better at solving the problems that life throws at you.

EXERCISE

This exercise will guide you through one of the problems that you want to work on. If you are getting stuck at any point you may find it helpful to refer back to the example of Elizabeth earlier in the chapter.

Describe the A (activating event – the situation that is causing you distress):

_____

_____

_____

_____

_____

_____

_____

_____

Using the table below, identify the B (belief system – self-talk, beliefs, etc.) that is maintaining your distress. Follow these instructions.

1 Read your problem again and try to listen to what you are telling yourself about it. They may be similar messages to those we identified for Elizabeth – it isn't fair, it should not have happened, they should not behave that way, etc. List these in the first table under 'Belief system (B) that is maintaining my distress'.

2 In the next table under 'Existing C' describe the consequences of your belief system, that is, how you currently feel about the problem you have described.

3 Next you need to think about how you would *like* to feel about your problem, the new C, your goal to aim for. What level of feelings would make it easier for you to deal with the problem you describe? How would you like to feel about it? This can be difficult, especially if in our opinion our feelings are strongly justified in view of how we have been treated. Think about how your family or friends, people that care about you, would want you to feel. We are not used to thinking about our emotions in this way, and one technique that sometimes is helpful is to try to measure the strength of your feelings. For example, supposing you are feeling very hurt about something. Try to rate the amount of

hurt you are feeling on a scale of 1 to 10, where 1 is no hurt and 10 is as hurt as you can imagine feeling. Say you rate yourself as 9 on the scale. Now think about what score you would like to feel and/or think it realistic to aim for. Remember you are looking for improvement, not necessarily perfection. You can use this technique to help you assess the level of distress you are experiencing for most of your feelings. It helps you to think more clearly about them.

1 _____ 10
(No   (Extremely
hurt)   hurt)

4 Once you have identified the new C, work backwards to see how you would need to change what you are currently telling yourself about the situation. Enter your new self-talk messages into the first table as your new belief system.

Belief system (B) that is maintaining my distress	New belief system required to positively change feelings and behaviour

Existing C: How I currently feel	New C: How I would like to feel

This exercise may take you a long time to complete, but do not get disheartened. Identifying what you are feeling and what you need to change about it is the core part of the process. You will find that the more you do this the easier it becomes. You are learning a useful technique that will enable you to become a better problem solver. If you are finding it difficult to complete the exercise for your major forgiveness problem, begin on something that you are less upset about. It does get much easier with practice. You become better at recognizing what you are telling yourself, how you are describing situations and how you are evaluating them. Once you have completed this exercise you can make your own cue cards with the new beliefs on them, that you can use as prompts when you find yourself in difficulty.

8

Dealing with anger

Anger is an emotion that most of us find particularly difficult to deal with. It is frequently our anger that gets in the way of forgiveness. This chapter explores in some detail how and why we get angry and deals with strategies that can help us to understand and cope better with our anger long term. The aim is not to prevent us from ever becoming angry – a totally unrealistic and even unhelpful goal for most of us. Anger is a natural response that at times can be quite useful. It can give us the courage to do and say things that perhaps need to be said but that we are normally reluctant to tackle.

However, most of us will at some time have been so angry that we have been unable to behave effectively. We can be speechless with anger, and only after the event can we think of what we should have said. This frequently makes us more annoyed. In other words, being angry can sometimes mean that we actually lose all control of a situation. This may then result in us being seen to be weak, and that may add to the difficulties we are experiencing. This is generally true of all extreme emotions, but anger in particular is most relevant to forgiveness. I want to introduce you to techniques that can help you get your anger under control more quickly. A knowledge of how your anger is created may help prevent you becoming angry or at least moderate your levels of anger. Experiencing sustained high levels of anger can be extremely damaging for our health and well-being. The aim here is to help you to come to terms with your anger and understand how you can begin to remove it.

At this point, some readers may say that they do not simply *get* angry, but that other people *make them* angry, and they have no control over this. Here we need to reconsider what we covered in Chapter 6. We established that everyone can choose how to behave, and this is also true of our feelings. We do have some control of how we feel. Other people cannot make us angry if we do not allow them to do so. People may talk about the human species as being naturally aggressive, and anger being a biological response, but the current consensus in psychology is that this is not necessarily the case. We may *learn* to be aggressive and to use emotional responses such as anger to manipulate others and to try to get our own way, and to be fair some people are more predisposed to use anger or react angrily than others, because of their personality. This is not a reason, however, for not trying to do something about our anger. Everyone can learn to have more control over their angry feelings.

Controlling anger

Therefore we begin this discussion from the position that we can all learn to control our emotions, including anger, but controlling anger for some people creates special difficulties. There are three thoughts that are especially important for our understanding of anger. The first is that in most instances, *other people cannot make us angry unless we choose to let them do so.* Second, *we can choose how angry to be about something, or indeed whether or not to be angry.* Third, *we can choose how long we continue to feel anger.* This latter point is often less acknowledged, yet it is crucial for our physical and psychological health. Maintaining your anger over long periods is very stressful and as we saw in Chapter 3, stress can be extremely damaging to our health.

These are revolutionary thoughts for those of us who believe that anger is something that is outwith our control. It is infinitely more comforting to blame others for making you angry than to accept some level of responsibility for your own anger.

Joyce was 34 and married. She had been a secretary prior to having her two children but was now a full-time mother. Her husband was an office manager. Their relationship was reasonably happy until the younger child went to nursery school. Since then Joyce said that her husband had been putting enormous pressure on her to return to work. She was resisting this, as she felt that the children still needed her to be there. Over the last few months it had become a huge bone of contention between them and their relationship was deteriorating as a result. Every evening her husband would come in from work and make some sarcastic comment about Joyce's life of leisure. She would respond angrily and a row would ensue. He would then invariably take himself off to the local pub saying something like, it was a sorry state of affairs when a man came home after a hard day's work and could not get any peace in his own home. His departure to the pub would make Joyce even more angry – before the children were born it had been his practice to stop at the pub on his way home every evening, and he had stopped doing this only after many arguments.

Joyce's view of events was that her husband 'wound her up' every evening. He came in and deliberately said things that would make her angry. Then he escalated things so that he could get his own way and go to the pub. As a result they never had a peaceful meal on week nights and their relationship was going downhill. She felt angry with him almost all the time and this was making her very irritable. Joyce was not very receptive initially to the idea that she was *allowing* her husband to 'wind her up'. Her view was that he was totally in the wrong and that every sane woman would agree. He was also possibly getting more out of the situation than her, as he went to the pub most evenings for a pleasant, quiet drink. She was aware, however, that he must know that it was damaging their relationship.

Her view was that he *must not* do it. She was demanding that he stop, and was getting extremely angry when he refused to do so. It was difficult for her to accept that we cannot dictate how other people behave – at best we can negotiate and reach a compromise. However their interaction on this topic seemed beyond negotiation: they had to stop rowing before being able to talk. Her husband saw it as her problem and he was unwilling to do anything about it. Joyce felt that the present situation could not continue, so the only option was for her to do something. It was against this background that she started to work on the problem.

An examination of her self-talk was interesting. It turned out that as soon as she heard the car in the drive, she was beginning to get angry, in anticipation of what he would say to her.

A: Joyce hears the car drawing up and her husband getting out and coming up the path, and she begins to anticipate what he is going to say.

B: (belief system that is maintaining my distress)
I wonder what he'll have to say today?
He has no idea what my life is like here with the kids and the housework.
How dare he suggest that I am idle and lazy?

I work hard and he should know it.
His food is always ready and the house is always clean.
He is really ungrateful.
He doesn't appreciate me and he should.
He just does it to wind me up so that he can go off to the pub
and feel no guilt about doing so.
He is a selfish b—.
(*And so on in this vein, with old hurts and grievances coming
into play.*)

From this self-talk it is apparent that Joyce is getting ready for a fight before her husband comes through the door. She is anticipating his remarks and preparing to respond angrily. By the time he delivers some comment about her 'life of leisure' she is already angry and answers him accordingly.

Until Joyce was asked to sit and think about her self-talk, she was not aware that she was actually doing this. As discussed earlier, self-talk is an unconscious process that occurs automatically – we are not aware that we are doing it. It can be quite difficult to 'tune' in to your own self-talk and I often suggest that people keep pen and paper to hand and note down what they are telling themselves as soon as it happens. Joyce had difficulties with this, and kept pen and paper in her downstairs toilet, just off her kitchen. When she found herself getting angry she would quickly withdraw to the toilet to examine her self-talk. It is not easy to recognize what you are telling yourself, but it is essential if you are to understand how you are getting yourself to become angry. You are describing the situation to yourself and you are evaluating it negatively: it should not be like this, they should not be behaving in that way, and so on.

The next step was for Joyce to think about how she *could* feel when her husband came home and delivered his 'wind up' comment. Initially Joyce could not envisage being anything other than angry. Here it might be useful to think about how other people might respond in this situation. Would everyone be angry? Joyce had to grudgingly admit that perhaps not everyone would be. One response would be not to care what he said; but if they wished to maintain their relationship this was probably not the best option. Perhaps she could be *amused* by him. At first she found this impossible to imagine, until she was asked to think about their typical evening interaction as if it were a sitcom on the television. This is a useful technique that helps to distance you from the emotion of the situation as you experience it. Imagine someone else telling you about it, or it happening to a friend, or watching it on television. Joyce began to see that it could seem slightly ridiculous and even funny to an observer. The same activity was repeated every evening, with the same outcome, in a crazy cycle. The next stage was to get Joyce to think about what she would need to be telling herself to begin to feel differently about the situation.

A: Joyce hears the car drawing up and her husband getting out and coming up the path, and she begins to anticipate what he is going to say.

New B: belief system required to positively change feelings and behaviour	New C: consequences (behaviour and feelings)
Here he comes again. He is really very predictable. I wonder what he'll have thought up today. It's really quite funny to think of him driving home thinking how he is going to try to wind me up. I refuse to be upset by it. I am not going to give him the satisfaction of getting angry. He knows really how hard I work. This situation has got out of hand and we have both said things we do not mean.	Fails to respond angrily to her husband's comment. Feeling that it is quite funny really especially as he is bemused by her failure to respond. Husband has no excuse to storm off to the pub in an angry huff.

Joyce began rehearsing her self-talk when she heard the car. She had them written down and kept them inside a kitchen drawer to remind herself, as the urge to respond angrily was very strong. Her husband's utter confusion at her failure to get annoyed and shout back at him, which then allowed him to take control of the situation and storm out, made her realize that by letting him make her angry, she had been allowing herself to be manipulated. She stopped giving him the power to 'make' her angry or 'wind her up'. This is a significant lesson. People cannot usually make you angry if you choose not to let them. This can be achieved, with work and commitment. It proved to be a turning-point for Joyce and her husband. He lost the power to manipulate her. Initially he responded by getting worse, trying even harder to make her angry but Joyce persevered, and found it became easier. Eventually they were able to talk about what was going on and finally reached a compromise with Joyce agreeing to do some part-time work in the future.

There are lessons to be learnt from this example that apply to forgiveness situations. The fundamental issue is that we cannot *demand* that other people behave differently or do certain things because *we* think that they should. People will generally do what they want to do, and at best we may hope to negotiate a compromise, where we both may get some of what we want. In Joyce's story, an important point in her self-talk was when she acknowledged to herself that her husband could not 'wind her up', he could only *try* to do it, and the choice of whether or not he succeeded was hers to make. You can think of this as taking back control. You are refusing to let the other person dictate how you feel and behave. This is particularly important in relation to bearing grudges and failing to forgive. Remember that by holding on to your anger at having been wronged, you are allowing the perpetrator to continue to hurt you.

Breaking the anger cycle

Anger related to having been wronged is frequently related to experiencing high levels of frustration. The victim feels powerless. They want something to happen – the perpetrator to be punished, some sort of retribution. However they do not usually have the power to achieve any of these things, and become very frustrated as a result. They are constantly thinking that *it should not be like this.*

There is also an expectation within themselves that they should be able to do something about it and not being able to achieve this can make people even angrier. Beck (1976) pointed out that anger can occur when our own personal rules, relating to how we expect to be treated by others, are violated. Notions of being respected by others, being treated politely, honestly and fairly come into play here. When we feel we have been badly wronged we become very angry. We have already discussed the belief that most of us cling to, despite all the evidence to the contrary, that the world should be a fair and just place. We tend to exhibit unhelpful levels of anger when we are treated unfairly, as we see it. Often we lash out and this commonly makes the situation worse.

What we are doing is demanding that other people, and the world in general, must be different. *Things should and indeed must be the way we want them to be.* But as we have seen, we do not have the power to demand things of others. Therefore, rather than expressing what we want as demands, if we can express them as wishes and preferences, then we will with practice stop getting so upset. At a very simple level in relation to forgiveness this goes as follows.

Current situation:

A: Experience of some wrong done to the victim.

B: It should not have happened. (*You have no control over this.*) They must be punished. (*Most times you do not have the power to ensure that this happens.*)

I demand that something be done. (*Again usually you do not have the power to do this.*)

It is unfair. (*It may be, but then so is life.*)

C: The victim is angry and upset. The anger continues to be fuelled by the frustration experienced when none of the victim's demands are met. This results in long-term anger and related distress, and psychological and physical damage to the victim of the kinds described earlier.

When we make demands about how we should be treated and how the world should be, it is no surprise that we can get really upset when our demands are not met. We have set up expectations that logically we know are not likely to be met, but we still demand that they should be, and therefore get very upset when they are not. To break the anger cycle, it is necessary for us to downgrade our demands to *preferences*. For example, it is certainly true, as we have seen, that we cannot demand that people treat us fairly but we certainly *prefer* it when they do. Reducing demands to preferences is a more accurate representation of what we can actually achieve in the real world. The crucial effect of this is that it does not create an expectation that what we *want* will necessarily *happen*. This can help to reduce our distress when things do not got our way. We can learn to become more philosophical about our disappointments and perceived mistreatment. An exploration of the corresponding ABC will make this clearer.

Current situation:
A: Experience of some wrong done to the victim.
B: These things do happen. It is distressing, but that is life.
   I know it is unfair, but then life is unfair.
   People do make mistakes from time to time and I am the victim of one of these mistakes.
   (*All anger-reducing thoughts.*)
C: The victim is upset and disappointed, but much less likely to be ineffectually angry.

The victim will not immediately feel this way, however. Most of us, including trained therapists, may feel the original angry response when some wrong is done to us. We are likely to respond to stress with anger. We feel anger at the time the event occurred, but we tend to actively maintain our anger by continuing to think about it. We rehearse our beliefs about what has happened and just by thinking about them we get angry. In the example of Joyce earlier, simply hearing her husband's car was enough to start her anger cycle. Hearing the perpetrator's name may set off your anger-inducing thoughts, or seeing one of their colleagues, or being near the place where the event happened. All sorts of triggers can set our train of anger-inducing thoughts in motion. With practice we can come to recognize them, and this is where our cue cards containing anger-reducing thoughts can be valuable. Carry these with you as an aid to combat the anger-inducing thoughts you are producing.

A helpful way of conceptualizing this process of change is to think of your self-talk as consisting of two voices inside your head. Initially the anger-inducing thoughts are loud and powerful. You introduce a second voice, that of the anger-reducing thoughts, and the two then battle for supremacy. Initially the anger-inducing thoughts are the loudest, but with practice the anger-reducing ones will come to dominate.

Frustration, either at our own inability to do anything about the situation or failure of others to punish the perpetrator, can be an additional trigger in anger related to non-forgiveness. In the same way, however, by thinking through and identifying the messages you are giving yourself in your self-talk, you can with practice break the frustration–anger cycle and bring your anger under control. You can then put your energies into dealing constructively with the problem and you will have minimized your distress levels. Getting your anger under control is necessary if you are to achieve forgiveness. It may not disappear, but it will reduce to more manageable levels. It may be transformed into a more general sadness and disappointment, and this happens commonly.

The message from this section is therefore that many of us need to alter some of the unwritten rules that we use to guide our behaviour. We have to regain control of our own emotional responses and stop allowing others to make us angry. We have to stop blaming others for making us angry and take responsibility for our own feelings. We have to accept that the world is not fair and just, and that people will not always treat us as we would like to be treated. We are trying to deal with things *as they are* and this will help us to give up our unrealistic expectations that are causing us problems. Achieving all of this does not mean that you will not get angry, but your levels of anger and the length of time the anger lasts will reduce. You will be able to control your anger and with practice be able to break the long-term cycles of anger that are so distressing and damaging to health.

EXERCISE

At this point it can be useful to revisit the anger problem you worked on in Chapter 6 (page 53). Think about a recent situation where you were *angry* and describe your anger-inducing self-talk.

Then, using the same A, think about how you would *like* to feel about the situation. What would be a comfortable level of feeling? Describe this under C in the second table.

DEALING WITH ANGER

Anger-inducing self-talk

A: activating event *What happened.*	B: beliefs about A and evaluations of A *How you described it to yourself and how you evaluated it.*	C: emotional and/or behavioural consequences *What you felt and what you did.*
		Anger.

Anger-reducing self-talk

A: activating event *What happened.*	B: new beliefs about A and new evaluations of A *How you need to describe it to yourself and evaluate it to reduce or remove your anger.*	C: emotional and/or behavioural consequences that you would like to feel.

9
Developing empathy

Empathy involves looking at the world through another person's eyes. It requires us to suspend our judgement of the person and try to understand why they have behaved as they have done. This is not easy at the best of times, and if that person has hurt or wronged us in some way it is even more difficult. However, despite this, there is evidence that when people come to forgive they do just this. As part of the process of coming to forgive, the victim begins to see how the perpetrator's behaviour may have seemed to *them*, what may have provoked their actions and even how they felt about it. This insight does not come all at once, but gradually victims come to realize that perhaps the perpetrator had not meant this to happen, or perhaps had not realized the full effect that their actions would have.

Understanding other people's motives

I can image that many of you reading this are already thinking, of course they did, they knew perfectly well what they were doing, they meant it all to happen, or other similar sentiments. Remember, as we have discussed, we all see the world differently. You will be aware that not everyone around you views your situation exactly the way you do. Friends may already have annoyed you by suggesting that perhaps things are not quite as you see them, perhaps implying that you have been harsh in your judgement.

At the outset it must be stated that developing empathy towards the perpetrator may not always be possible. Sometimes people do behave very badly and it is hard to find reasons to excuse their behaviour. People do some very evil things and most of us are not able to understand why they do them. In such cases it would be impossible for us to put ourselves in their shoes and view the world through their eyes. Their behaviour is so far removed from our idea of what is acceptable that empathy is impossible. But I would argue that these in the main are the exceptions. Even when people behave in ways that we believe we would never contemplate behaving ourselves, we may come to understand what has driven them to that behaviour. As human beings we are capable of demonstrating enormous understanding for others.

In the early years of my professional life, I felt that I would find it very difficult, if not impossible, to work with parents who had abused their children as I would not be able to be empathic. However, when I found myself in the position of having to do this it did not prove to be too hard to understand why some of these parents acted as they did. Perhaps they were living in very difficult circumstances, with little support and very little money, and the constant demands of a fretful baby, together with their own tiredness, drove them to breaking point on occasions. Perhaps they had experienced deprivation in their own upbringing and had little sense of what parenting was about. Understanding where someone is coming from does not mean that you approve of their behaviour, merely that you try to suspend judgement to some extent.

As part of the process of working towards forgiveness, we need to try to see the perpetrator's point of view and to understand what their motivation might have been. A useful starting point here is to think about our own behaviour and that of other people we know. All of us would accept that every single person makes mistakes at sometime or another. Human beings by their very nature are prone to making mistakes. Every day we are presented with opportunities where we have to make choices. With every situation we inevitably run the risk of getting it wrong. Add to this the complexity of our lives, where we are frequently called upon to make instant decisions with only an incomplete understanding of the facts. When you really look at this complexity it is surprising that we do not get it wrong more often than we do. We need to remind ourselves, as a result, that *we are all fallible human beings*. Making mistakes is part of being human.

I would like you to reflect as honestly as you can on your own life. Have you ever jumped to a conclusion that was later shown to be wrong? Have you ever judged someone without knowing all the facts and then later realized that you were unfair on them? Have you ever done anything you were later ashamed of? Have you acted unwisely in the heat of the moment and then regretted it? I am sure by now we can all recall some situation where, on reflection, we have not behaved as we would have liked. We have all made mistakes because of the pressures we are under.

It might have been going along with some group decision or a comment made by friends or colleagues that later we think may have been unfair. After thinking about it we may feel that we should have taken the time or made the effort to disagree, but it seemed simpler to go along with the group. We may have acted in total ignorance of the harm that followed from our actions. We truly did not intend to hurt anyone.

I feel sure that none of us has gone through life without ever committing any errors of judgement, however well-meaning we think we are, and the more quick-tempered we are generally the more this may be true of us. We all do and say things in anger that we later regret. What we said might have been true, but on reflection we realize that it would have been kinder, or wiser, not to have said it.

So we acknowledge that we have made mistakes in our life. We have acted unwisely, unfairly or made harsh judgements. Next, we have to allow that this also happens to other people. Other people are also fallible human beings with their own pressures. They, like us, may make decisions and take actions hastily without having considered the implications. It may not have crossed their minds how you would feel about what they did or said. Perhaps they felt they acted in an appropriate manner, without thinking about the consequences. We have all acted on the spur of the moment. They may have been angry and simply lashed out. We need to accept that the excuses *we* give for the way *we* sometimes behave may also apply to other people. While some people in life do set out to be nasty and difficult, they are generally in the minority – most people do not deliberately go out of their way to hurt or otherwise damage others.

The perpetrator's point of view

It is very difficult, however, to try to think like the perpetrator. We need to ask, what was their motivation? We know what we believe it to have been, but is that the only possible cause of their behaviour? Is there a less damaging explanation? Did they really set out to deliberately harm you? Did they plan it that way? What do other people seem to think? What 'excuses' have they or others offered for their behaviour? Is it possible that some of these 'excuses' could have some truth in them?

EXERCISE

Refer back to the event you described at the end of Chapter 2 (page 16), where you felt that someone had behaved badly towards you. Go over your responses again, paying particular attention to the answers to questions 3 and 9. Copy your description of the event and your answers to these questions below.

Describe the event where you felt someone wronged you (from Chapter 2).

_____

_____

_____

_____

_____

_____

How intentional was the act? Mark the appropriate point on the line. (Question 3 from page 17.)

Totally
premeditated _____ Accidental

Can you think of any reasons that might help to explain the way the perpetrator behaved towards you? Note them down. (Question 9 from page 17.)

_____

_____

_____

_____

_____

_____

When first asked to think of reasons why someone has wronged them, most people provide statements that in some way confirm that the behaviour was intentional, or at least designed in some way to directly cause harm to them. Try to revisit this. Ask the questions we posed above. How might the perpetrator describe their behaviour? What excuses might they offer? Are they perhaps themselves somehow 'damaged' so that they find it difficult to behave in any other way? This can be the case with some types of extreme behaviour. You really need to suspend your judgement at this point. Simply try to come up with possible reasons to explain the way the perpetrator behaved towards you. Write them down below, even the most far-fetched and unlikely ones. Do not judge whether or not they are likely to be true. Just write them down. Remember that people can often behave very stupidly and irresponsibly without really meaning to do anyone any harm.

_____

_____

_____

_____

_____

_____

Interpreting events differently

By completing this exercise you have made another major step towards being able to forgive. Keep reminding yourself that people often do stupid things and can act very irresponsibly without ever really meaning to do anyone any harm. Sometimes things do simply happen by chance. People can be unfortunate enough to be in the wrong place at the wrong time.

Most victims can come up with possible reasons why the perpetrator acted as they did. Whether or not you believe any of them at this point is another matter. You have made a significant breakthrough by allowing yourself to acknowledge that they may see the situation differently from you. You are attempting to see the world through their eyes, to be empathic, to allow that your way of seeing and judging situations is perhaps not the only one.

What you are doing here is acknowledging that things may be more complex than or very different from the way you initially judged them to be. You are allowing that your interpretation may not have been totally accurate, or if you are still convinced about this, you are allowing that the other person's reasons for acting as they did may be different from your original understanding. It may be, as mentionied earlier, that while you cannot understand them, you can now see that they are very unhappy people, more to be pitied than hated. You are allowing space for the idea that forgiveness just might be a possibility, or at the very least that you can 'get over' this event and carry on with your life.

Victims often find this a painful, difficult process, and some respond by questioning whether they really have to go through this. If you are feeling this way, remember the dangers of non-forgiveness, of continuing to be angry, bearing a grudge. You may be damaging your health, your relationships with others and your future happiness by clinging on to your anger. Do you really want to continue to allow the perpetrator to affect you in this way?

The possibility of forgiveness

If the perpetrator is someone you care about and have previously had a good relationship with, it can be helpful to recall the good experiences you had together. It is tempting to do this in a judgemental way, but this is not helpful. If you find yourself recalling previous good times with the person and then saying to yourself, for example, 'Imagine treating me like this after what we meant to each other, how dare she? All I ever showed her was kindness,' and so on, then you need to be aware of the effect your self-talk is having.

It is time to return to the ABC model. In the table below I show how your self-talk needs to change if you are to appreciate what might be the perpetrator's motivation and their understanding of the situation. Example 1 illustrates how we maintain our unforgiving attitudes, while example 2 shows that by reflecting on previous good experiences and trying to be less judgemental in your self-talk, you can begin to allow the possibility of forgiveness.

Every situation will, of course, be different but the principles remain the same. Try to recognize what you are telling yourself that is resulting in your current feelings. You may find that writing this down helps you to get it straight. If you are being judgemental, think about how you would have to change your self-talk to avoid this. Explore how this then makes you feel.

Once they get the hang of this, most people find it a worthwhile exercise. With continued practice you will become more insightful about your feelings and ultimately have more control over how you think, feel and behave. It will become easier to choose to forgive, should you decide that this is what you want.

A: activating event	B: what you believe about the situation, your self-talk	C: emotional and /or behavioural consequences
Example 1 Thinking of previous good experiences with the person.	How dare she do this after the way we were friends for so long? All I showed her was kindness. She should not have done it.	Anger Sadness Indignation (*Unforgiving*)
Example 2 Thinking of previous good experiences with the person.	We have had good times together in the past. She has previously been a good friend. She can't be that bad, otherwise why did I choose her as a friend?	Lessening of negative emotions. Some sadness about what has happened. Beginnings of empathic understanding. Allowing that at some future point

	Of course she had lots of positive qualities. I would lose a lot if we were never to be friends again. Perhaps it was not quite as bad as I thought? I can see that it looked a little different from her point of view. Perhaps she did not really intend for me to be hurt?	forgiveness just might be possible.

10

The transformation of forgiveness

By working through this difficult situation, you are in fact being very generous. You may feel that you were badly wronged and treated unjustly, but trying to understand what motivated the perpetrator and to see whether this makes their behaviour less unacceptable is a very generous act. You are rising above the situation and acting in a brave and honourable manner. No one can insist that you forgive someone who has wronged you, but as we have seen it is unwise for your own health and well-being to remain angry and upset and allow the perpetrator to continue to hurt you.

Deciding to forgive

True forgiveness is not easily achieved. The process normally begins once the shock is over and the initial anger and hurt have died down a little, or perhaps the victim has learned to live with them or has some control over them, often by using the techniques described earlier in the book. When someone states they will forgive another person, what they are usually really saying is that they would *like* to forgive the person and are willing to *try* to forgive them. They are committing themselves to begin the process of forgiveness. This can be described as victims 'having a change of heart'. They decide, often quite suddenly, that nothing more is to be gained by sticking with the current situation. They may say that they have forgiven the perpetrator. However, a statement of forgiveness does not mean that forgiveness has been achieved. Working with couples where one partner has been unfaithful bears witness to this. The 'guilty' party assumes they have been forgiven, and expects things to return to normal, as though the incident had not occurred. However, the 'wronged' party continues to act in ways intended to punish their partner and make them feel guilty. The 'guilty' party complains about never being allowed to forget, and the relationship may deteriorate further. What the victim actually meant was that they would *try* to forgive them. They have made a commitment to forgive, but this is only the first, albeit crucial, stage of forgiveness. There is some way to go before true forgiveness is achieved.

Generally, by the time the commitment is made, the feelings of hurt and anger are greatly reduced. There may be some empathic understanding of the perpetrator's motives. Some change in your feelings towards the offender will be taking place, but almost without you really being aware of it. It may be a platitude, but the saying, time is a great healer, has much truth in it. You will have talked through the situation and gone over it in your mind, and you will have begun to come to terms with what has happened. You may find yourself occasionally starting to think that perhaps the perpetrator is not quite as bad as you thought they were or that the situation is rather more complex than you first assumed. This is all part of the process of beginning to work at forgiveness. You are starting to describe the event slightly differently, reflecting your changing views.

At this point victims frequently reflect on their own behaviour, reminding themselves that, like the perpetrator, they are not perfect. You may never have committed the magnitude of offence that you have suffered, but it is unlikely that any of us has not caused offence at some point in our lives.

We may reflect on how we have coped with what happened to us, and we may feel somewhat embarrassed about our own failings in this respect. Perhaps we made a great fuss, and in retrospect we see that we may have overreacted a little. Perhaps the event was not quite as awful as we made it out to be.

Feelings like these, and an acknowledgement that we are not totally blame-free in our own lives can make us feel a little guilty about our own contribution to the event. This is certainly true in cases of interpersonal events with people we have previously had reasonable relationships with. Here I focus on the types of situations where forgiveness is more easily achieved. When individuals experience major losses and the associated pain caused by strangers or events totally outwith their control, it is often more difficult to come to terms with the situation and contemplate forgiveness. These problematic situations will be discussed in more detail in the next chapter.

Guilt as a motivation to forgive

Guilt is a wonderful motivator. When we are feeling guilty about something it tends to eat away at us, provoking us until we do something about it. A feeling of guilt (although this admittedly may be only slight) about our continuing failure to forgive is important in keeping us working towards granting forgiveness. It is helpful here to think of situations where you have done something wrong and been forgiven. We can all recall such events, perhaps from our childhood. It is a very humbling experience to admit to yourself that you have caused hurt to other people in the past. A useful exercise here is to write about the experience, including what it was like to be forgiven.

EXERCISE

Write down brief details of an event where you were forgiven, and try to remember how you felt about it at the time.

_____

_____

_____

_____

_____

_____

_____

Now try to recall how it felt when you were forgiven. Think also about how you felt about the person/people who forgave you.

_____

_____

_____

_____

_____

_____

_____

_____

_____

Did you feel you deserved to be forgiven? Explore why you felt that way.

_____

_____

_____

_____

_____

_____

_____

_____

The perpetrators need to be forgiven

For most of us the experience of being forgiven brings with it a great sense of relief, and gratitude towards the person who has forgiven us. It is a good feeling. The relief we feel makes us realize that as a wrongdoer we also suffered. Up to this point it is common for victims to assume that they are the only people who are suffering, whereas it is frequently the case that the perpetrator is also suffering. They may be feeling guilty, aggrieved, hurt, misunderstood, depending on how they have interpreted the situation. This will not always be the case, but often the wrongdoer will not be feeling comfortable about the situation. They feel the need to be forgiven, even if they are too stubborn to admit it. Remember that the majority of people do not go out of their way to hurt or offend others. Life is pleasanter for all of us when we interact without friction.

It is also useful to consider that just as you, the victim, have been going through the process of reinterpreting the situation, the same is likely to apply to the offender. They too may have queried their own behaviour. Questions such as whether they have been mistaken in their views of things, or whether they should have acted as they did are very likely to have entered their minds.

Forgiveness as a gift

The last exercise you did had three aims. The first was to make you really think about an incident where you required forgiveness. Doing this does make us very aware of our own imperfections and can help us to be more tolerant of those of others. Second, it allowed you to recall exactly what it feels like to be forgiven. It is a good feeling that can also be humbling, especially if you felt you did not really deserve forgiveness. Third, it made you think about your feelings towards the person who forgave you. The individual who has forgiven someone, especially if that person feels they do not deserve to be forgiven, is viewed very positively, as someone who is trying to put things right. We see such people as having a generous spirit, as being able to rise above things, take the knocks and get on with life. This last point holds one of the keys to understanding the process of forgiveness. *Forgiveness is perhaps best understood as a gift that you can give to the perpetrator.*

This may seem a strange way to view forgiveness. More prevalent is the traditional view that forgiveness has to be earned. We commonly believe that people should suffer for their sins. People who have behaved badly should be punished, and this is especially true of those who have offended against us. However, as we have seen, in most instances the offender will also be suffering. In all probability it will have made their life more difficult, especially if you are moving in the same social circles. Usually a perpetrator does not suffer as much as their victim, or the victim may feel that they do not, and this is why forgiveness is in essence a gift that the victim can bestow on the offender. It does not matter if others think that they do not deserve it. It can be an even more powerful gift when it is given in these circumstances.

If you recall a situation where you were forgiven although you felt you did not deserve it, undoubtedly you thought a great deal of the person bestowing forgiveness. The lesson you are teaching when you forgive is about the generosity of the human spirit. People can do good even in the face of wrongdoing. The person that is forgiven is likely to experience a heightened sense of guilt, which may be an element of punishment. This may make them want to be more co-operative. Hopefully they will also have learnt some valuable lessons about the rules of social interaction. You have the freedom to choose to forgive, and actually forgiving can be a very positive experience that will help to counterbalance all the pain that has gone before. It is a very emotional event to forgive someone.

Forgiving someone does not necessarily mean that you publicly acknowledge that you have done so. You can forgive someone without ever letting them know about it. You can forgive someone you no longer have any contact with or someone who has died. The main point of forgiveness is to make *you* feel better, to remove some of the stress from your life and allow you to stop dwelling on the hurt and move on.

When we looked at the benefits of not forgiving (page 21), we saw that this means that we can avoid, or minimize, contact with the perpetrator, and this makes us feel less anxious as they cannot hurt us again. Once you forgive someone and resume contact with them you are leaving yourself open to that possibility. This is why it is a brave and generous act. Realistically it is very unlikely that they will set out to deliberately hurt you again, because of their own uncomfortable feelings. They are more likely to be careful in their interactions with you for some time. They may actively try to make amends.

Is an apology necessary?

One question that often arises is whether there needs to be an admission of guilt and an apology from the perpetrator before forgiveness can be granted. In an ideal world wrongdoers would admit their guilt and apologize, and then be forgiven. Unfortunately as we know this doesn't often happen. But there are real benefits to be had in forgiveness even where no admission of guilt or apology is forthcoming. It will make resuming normal interactions with the perpetrator somewhat more difficult but it can be done.

Jennifer was falsely accused of something by Samantha, a work colleague, someone she had thought of as a friend. After an investigation the false nature of the allegations became apparent, but Jennifer had found the whole process extremely stressful. She expected an apology from Samantha but none was forthcoming and no action was taken at work to mediate in the situation. The view was that staff could raise their concerns freely. They would be investigated and it would all be done impartially. Jennifer really loved her job and was reluctant to leave but could not see how she could continue to work alongside Samantha. She was incensed at the unfairness of the situation, as she perceived it.

After working through her feelings, she came to see that she could still work in the organization as she had only a minimal public interaction with Samantha, at occasional meetings. She had interacted with her more frequently previously, as she had thought they were friends, but she came to see that to do her job effectively and enjoyably she did not need this contact.

She finally came to view the situation as having taught her useful lessons. She saw that Samantha had lost a good friend in herself, but she was very determined not to let the event cause her any more distress or interfere with her enjoyment of work. She bore no grudge and wrote it off as a painful but useful experience. When the situation demanded, she behaved very professionally with Samantha, and indeed found that Samantha seemed more uncomfortable with the situation than she now was.

Many people have great difficulty apologizing for things that they have done. They may simply be very stubborn, or not confident enough to bear the 'loss of face' involved in admitting they were wrong and saying sorry. Just as it takes courage to forgive someone, it also takes courage to admit that you were wrong. Again it is acknowledging that you are a fallible human being just like other people, who makes mistakes. When people apologize, though, we tend to think well of them. You hear people talk of someone being 'big enough' to admit their mistake and apologize. It can be helpful in the absence of an acceptance of any degree of responsibility for the wrongdoing to see that as being the perpetrator's problem. You cannot demand that anyone apologize and it is pointless to get upset if no apology is forthcoming. That will only affect you – it will make you stressed and will bring you no closer to getting your apology. Here again you need to examine your self-talk to minimize your distress. The following example may help you with this.

A: activating event	B: what you believe about the situation, your self-talk	C: emotional and /or behavioural consequences
Example 1 Apology is not forthcoming.	She should apologize. She is clearly in the wrong. I am owed an apology.	Anger. Indignation. (*Unforgiving.*)
Example 2 Apology is not forthcoming.	I can't make her apologize. It would be good if she would apologize and it is a little sad that she is not big enough to do so. At the end of the day I don't suppose it would make much difference. What happened happened and I am putting it behind me and getting on with my life.	Acceptance of the situation. Lessening of negative emotions, perhaps some sadness about what has happened. Forgiveness possible.

By working through your feelings about the lack of an admission of guilt or apology you can come to the point where it does not upset you. Undoubtedly it is easier to forgive if someone has apologized, even if you do not totally agree about who was most to blame for the event. An

103

apology can signal closure of the event and allow both parties to move on. An apology does not cancel out what has happened, but it may help to restore some balance in the relationship between the two parties. We know that it is not easy to admit guilt and apologize. The perpetrator makes a commitment to the victim when they apologize; by accepting the apology the victim makes a commitment to work towards forgiveness.

Positive outcomes

Once forgiveness has been given, as part of the process the victim often tends to redefine the situation and look for some positive things that may have come out of it. This is about making it a more positive experience, both for you and for others. It is about trying to see that, despite all the pain, something good has come out of the situation in the end. Commonly people say that in some way it has made them a better person. They may be more sympathetic to others and more sensitive in their interactions. For example, Jennifer (page 101) came to see that she had learnt valuable lessons. She felt that she was a wiser person as a result and that she had defined her professional role in the workplace more effectively.

Other people report that going through the process of learning to forgive has given them insight into their own behaviour and they feel more confident in themselves as a result. Many are profoundly changed by the experience, especially when it involves the forgiveness of something fairly major. They report that they see life somewhat differently, are more philosophical, and get less upset by similar situations when they arise. There is a general consensus that once someone has forgiven it is never quite so difficult to do it again. This may be partly explained by the feelings of relief and closure that accompany real forgiveness. There is a sense of completion, of putting the past behind you and of being able to get on with life again. You will feel better as a result of having removed a significant source of stress from your life, and from the knowledge that you have done a brave and generous thing.

Forgiving is not forgetting

As a final footnote on achieving true forgiveness, it is important to state that most victims make a clear distinction between forgiving and forgetting. The majority stress that while they may have forgiven they have not forgotten. The memory of the event seems to act as a warning trigger for them in their interactions with the individual. By forgiving the perpetrator they are leaving themselves open to being hurt by them again. The memory of the hurt makes them more wary in their interactions with that individual. Their trust has been violated, and it seems that it takes some time for that trust to be built up again. This is commonly observed where there has been infidelity in a relationship. There may be reconciliation but the level of suspicion of the victim tends to remain high for some time. That people learn to trust again is evidence of the resilience and the generosity of human beings. Forgiveness brings positive benefits to the person who forgives but also to those who are forgiven.

11

When true forgiveness is not possible

How easy it is to achieve forgiveness will depend to some extent on the nature of the wrongdoing. This is not a direct relationship, however, and research shows that some people are more forgiving by nature than are others. People's propensity to forgive varies, and this is also influenced by social and cultural factors and practices. Non-forgiveness, as we have seen, carries with it great costs to the individual in terms of health and happiness. The perpetrator is still exacting a toll on the victim as long as the victim is suffering the effects of the wrongdoing. In this chapter we look at ways of containing the damage to the victim. Where true forgiveness is not possible, due to the nature of the offence or the personality of the individual, we concentrate on how to draw a line under the event and move on.

An unrealistic goal

There are some types of event that people find difficult or impossible to forgive. One of these is where children are seriously injured or killed. There is an expectation that parents will die before their children, and when this is violated by the death of a child it can be very difficult to come to terms with. There are no easy answers here, or indeed for any situation involving the loss of loved ones. There seems to be a tendency to want to blame someone, a feeling that someone must pay. Again, to say that time is a great healer is telling the truth. For most people the pain eventually gets easier to bear although it is unlikely ever to go away totally. As part of coming to terms with the events, some people work hard to give them some positive meaning. They may say something to the effect that they want to ensure that their son's death was not in vain. They may get involved in charitable work or political campaigning activities in an attempt to prevent a similar occurrence in the future, or at least make some positive contribution. It is about getting something positive and meaningful out of the situation.

The need for retribution is very common and our legal system currently seems to encourage this. We no longer accept that accidents can happen. Someone always has to be to blame and damages extracted. However, this need for retribution and for justice to be seen to be done can be very destructive, as it can come to dominate an individual's life. It can stop them engaging with the future and leave them feeling very unhappy. The bottom line is that no amount of compensation can undo the situation. It is quite easy to become focused on the settlement of a court case as being the 'solution' of an event, but this is often not the case. People may be upset at the amount of the award they receive, with statements like, 'Is this all they think her life was worth?' On the surface it may seem a calculating or greedy remark, but sometimes what they are really saying is that they are still hurting. Getting the money has not made their hurt go away, it was not a solution. It may help deal with the practicalities of life, but it does not make the pain go away.

Court cases can drag on for some time and people going through this process talk about being in limbo, as if their life is on hold until the case is settled. This suspension of normal activities often also extends to their adjustment to their situation. A pending court case is an additional stressor and it does not foster the resolution of an individual's distress. Continuing to rehearse and conceptualize the events within a legal system that requires blame to be apportioned can be detrimental when trying to come to terms with a situation. Under normal circumstances we begin to come to terms with events with the passing of time, but court cases often extending over several years can significantly disrupt this process. This is not to argue that individuals should not seek justice through the legal system, merely to point out that receiving a settlement is unlikely to be a total solution.

Where offenders are caught and sent to prison, the victim frequently expresses some satisfaction that justice has been seen to be done. They may be very relieved that the perpetrator is no longer free to repeat their offences, but they still have to cope with their own pain relating to the event. After such trials, journalists often ask victims how they feel about the sentence, and the answers can be very interesting. People tend to look startled by the question, as if they are unsure of their feelings; sometimes there is disappointment at the length of sentence, or they comment that they simply want to get on with their life now. These comments reflect the realization that while the offender being sent to prison brings some satisfaction it is not a solution for their pain and the adjustment that they have to make. It is only part of the solution, and the victim still has to deal with their feelings towards the offender. Does knowing that the offender has been punished help you to forgive him or her? For some people it may be sufficient, but for many it has little effect, as they are still distressed and unable to pick up the pieces of their life and move on.

In these circumstances forgiveness may be an unrealistic goal. The task is to help the victim contain their distress, draw a line and move on. In my experience the strongest argument that can persuade the victim to stop focusing on the event is that the person who died or was injured would not have wanted them to be miserable for the rest of their life. One life has been cut short by the deed; it need not be two. Most individuals cannot disagree with this sentiment, and it can provide sufficient motivation to encourage them to try to engage with their life again.

Ways to reduce the distress

If all the strategies described earlier for working towards achieving forgiveness fail, all is not lost, however. There are still ways of minimizing distress. It is important to begin by looking at the messages the victim may be giving to themselves. The ABC formula can help here to explore typical self-talk in this situation. The first example below is of self-talk that keeps the individual focusing on the event and unable to move on. The second shows the changes that need to be made to their self-talk to enable them to change their feelings and allow them to move on.

These are very typical examples of the self-talk that people use in these situations. In the first example the crucial message is that the victim says that they will never forgive. This can become a self-fulfilling prophecy. Tell yourself something often enough and you will come to believe that it is true. By repeating this message to ourselves we come to believe it and it becomes the dominant 'voice' in our self-talk. Victims become highly practised at sending themselves the same messages and they have to work hard to change. All the techniques described earlier, such as cue cards and rehearsal are needed. It is not an easy task. Changing the core parts of our self-talk is equivalent to giving up a bad habit, and we all

A: activating event	B: what you believe about the situation, your self-talk	C: emotional and/or behavioural consequences
Think of the wrong suffered.	It should never have happened. I will never come to terms with this. I will never let it go. I will never forgive X.	Anger. Indignation. Unforgiving. *Unable to move on with life.*
Think of the wrong suffered.	I wish it had not happened but it did and nothing can change that. My loved one would not have wanted me to go on being unhappy. While I will never forgive X, I owe it to my loved ones to try to pick up the pieces. *Or* X has hurt me badly once, but I am not going to let them ruin the rest of my life.	Acceptance of the situation. Lessening of negative emotions, sadness and regret about what has happened. Unforgiving, but crucially *able to begin to move on with life.*

know how difficult that can be. It takes lots of practice and continued effort but the gains are worth it.

Individuals will have an inkling of how much change is possible in themselves. It is about making a choice about how you want to feel, not passively letting the perpetrator continue to dictate how you feel. Basically it is about regaining control of your feelings and ultimately your life. You may decide that the perpetrator does not deserve to be forgiven, and that is fine, it is your choice and you are free to make it. There are no value judgements here; it is a personal decision that you have the right to make. Forgiveness is a gift and you can choose not to bestow it if you feel it is undeserved. But you owe it to yourself to draw a line under the event, stop making it the focus of your life, and begin to pick up the pieces and move on.

Epilogue

Self-forgiveness

Throughout this book the focus has been on interpersonal forgiveness. The discussion has been about situations with a victim and a perpetrator. There are instances, however, where forgiveness is not about forgiving others but about forgiving ourselves. We are all fallible human beings. Few of us can have gone through life without doing some things we later regret. This is certainly the case for at least one of the parties, the wrongdoer, discussed in this book. But it would be remiss to conclude this discussion without a brief mention of self-forgiveness.

While it is only right that we should acknowledge our own mistakes, hopefully learn from them and move on, when it comes to blaming ourselves and carrying guilt, all the arguments made earlier about the dangers inherent in non-forgiveness of others also actually apply to non-forgiveness of self. It is very damaging to our physical and psychological health to excessively blame ourselves and feel guilty. If we do this we are significantly increasing the chances that we will fail to engage with life and ultimately become depressed. All the approaches and techniques discussed with reference to the forgiveness of others can actually be applied to the forgiveness of self.

One additional difficulty with the way that we judge ourselves is that we often tend to make harsher judgements about our own guilt than we do about others'. We make excuses for our friends' behaviour, but do not apply these same excuses to our own. It is very useful, when considering issues related to self-forgiveness, to try viewing the events as if they were happening to someone else. Imagine that a friend is telling you about it. Write down the details to get some distance from it and focus on the advice you would give to a friend. We are good at giving advice to other people, but sadly we do not always apply that advice when it is our own problem. We need to acknowledge that blaming ourselves excessively is self-defeating. All our energies go into maintaining the blaming instead of trying to improve the situation. We can all choose to be different,

111

even though we often seem to forget this. Change is never easy but it is usually worthwhile.

My aim in writing this book is to help individuals deal more effectively with their pain. The world is a very imperfect place. Human suffering abounds, and we can often do little about it. Where we *can* make a difference and relieve suffering, whether for ourselves or for others, I think we owe it to ourselves to try to make it happen. I hope that this book may go some little way to help you with this in your life.

References

Hans Seyle, *Stress in Health and Disease*, Reading, MA, Butterworth, 1976.
Aaron Beck, *Cognitive Therapy and the Emotional Disorders*, New York, International Universities Press, 1976.

Further reading

Dr Windy Dryden, *Overcoming Anger*, London, Sheldon Press, 1996.

Dr Windy Dryden, *Overcoming Guilt*, London, Sheldon Press, 1994.

Albert Ellis and Robert A. Harper, *A New Guide to Rational Living*, California, Wilshire Book Company, 1975.

Mary Hartley, *Managing Anger at Work*, London, Sheldon Press, 2002.

Index